Not Exactly What They Expected

Other Works by Al Hill

Our Evil—God's Good
And Other Sermons from Genesis through Judges

Things That Kings Can't Do
And Other Sermons from Judges through 2nd Kings, and the Wisdom Books

In the Presence of the Lord
And Other Sermons from the Psalms and the Prophets

Walking with Jesus
And Other Sermons from the Gospel of Matthew

God's Purpose for Your Faith
And Other Sermons from the Gospel of Mark, Hebrews, James and 1st Peter

From Jerusalem to Jericho
And Other Sermons from the Gospel of Luke and the Acts of the Apostles

Traits of the Shepherd
And Other Sermons from the Gospel of John, 1st John and Revelation

Making Peace with Your Father
And Other Sermons from Paul's Letters to the Romans and Corinthians

The Empty God
And Other Sermons from the Shorter Letters of Paul

O Come, Let God Adore Us
And Other Sermons for Advent and Christmas

Dear Trinity
Letters from a Pastor to His People

Not Exactly What They Expected
And Other Sermons for Holy Week and Easter

Al Hill

SUMMERTON
HOUSE

Copyright © 2018 Al Hill

All rights reserved. No part of this book may be used or reproduced by any means, graphic, electronic, or mechanical, including photocopying, recording, taping or by any information storage retrieval system without the written permission of the author except in the case of brief quotations embedded in critical articles and reviews.

Scripture quotations marked "KJV" are from the King James Version of the Bible.

Scripture quotations marked "RSV" are from the Revised Standard Version of the Bible, copyright © 1946, 1952, and 1971 by the National Council of the Churches of Christ in the United States of America. Used by permission. All rights reserved.

Scripture quotations marked "NIV" are from the Holy Bible, New International Version®, NIV®, copyright © 1973, 1978, 1984, and 2011 by Biblica, Inc.™ Used by permission of Zondervan. All rights reserved worldwide.

Scripture quotations marked "NKJV" are from taken the New King James Version®. Copyright © 1982 by Thomas Nelson. Used by permission. All rights reserved.

Scripture quotations marked "NRSV" are from the New Revised Standard Bible, copyright © 1989 by the National Council of the Churches of Christ in the United States of America. Used by permission. All rights reserved.

Scripture quotations marked "ESV" are from the ESV® Bible (The Holy Bible, English Standard Version®), copyright © 2001 by Crossway, a publishing ministry of Good News Publishers. Used by permission. All rights reserved.

Because of the dynamic nature of the Internet, any web addresses or links contained in this book may have changed since publication and may no longer be valid.

Cover design by the author.
Certain stock imagery © Shutterstock.

The Ascension window was created by Franz Xavier Zettler (1841 – 1916) and is located in The German Church (St. Gertrude's) in Stockholm, Sweden.

ISBN: 978-1-948773-09-6 (sc)

Library of Congress Control Number: 2018903361

To learn more about and purchase other works by Al Hill,
go to www.sommertonhouse.com
or www.amazon.com/author/alhill.

Dedication

To Michelle and Tim—
Michelle, a young and vibrant wife and mother
who was stricken with a terrible illness
that slowly robbed her body of its most basic abilities
and, finally, of life itself—
and Tim, her loving husband,
who served as her devoted caregiver,
through it all and to the end.

To bear her great burden,
Michelle needed more spiritual strength and hope
than my messages at the time were providing.
And one day she told me so.

Had it not been for her (justified) complaint
about the inadequacy of my preaching
that Sunday so many years ago,
the sermons in this book—
and many others—
would never have been written.

I could not understand
the words Michelle was trying so hard to utter that day,
but Tim patiently "interpreted" for me,
and in that sacred moment,
God spoke to me through them both.

Contents

Dedication v
Preface ix

Sermons

For Palm Sunday
Chapter 1. Not Exactly What They Expected 5
Chapter 2. They Could Not Keep Him Out 15
Chapter 3. Look Who's Here 25

For Maundy Thursday
Chapter 4. A Meal to Remember 35
Chapter 5. Delivery Charges 41
Chapter 6. Let's Try This Again 49
Chapter 7. I Serve You; I Command You 57
Chapter 8. A Very Difficult Commandment 61
Chapter 9. Treachery at the Table 69
Chapter 10. Hope in the Darkness 75

For Good Friday
Chapter 11. Trying Questions 87
Chapter 12. Our Evil—God's Good 97
Chapter 13. Who *Is* This Guy? 107
Chapter 14. This is Jesus 115
Chapter 15. Hanging Out with Jesus 121
Chapter 16. What Does It Take…? 129
Chapter 17. Learning Obedience 135
Chapter 18. The Empty God 139

For Easter
Chapter 19. The Believe It or Not Story 147
Chapter 20. Easter Come and Easter Go 153
Chapter 21. Have They Taken Away Your Lord? 157
Chapter 22. Today's the Day! 161
Chapter 23. You Can Kill Him, But… 167
Chapter 24. Life, If You Will Have It 177
Chapter 25. His Resurrection—and Yours 185
Chapter 26. Coming to Life—Again 195
Chapter 27. Hope, Grief and Joy 205

For the Sunday After Easter
Chapter 28. Unless I See Him 213
Chapter 29. For Want of a Resurrection… 217

Indices
Sermon Titles in Alphabetical Order 224
Sermon Texts in Biblical Order 226
Sermon Texts in Lectionary Order 229
Additional Scriptures Referenced 232

Preface

From birth to death—and beyond—Jesus was a Man Who confounded the expectations of friend and foe alike. And nowhere was this more apparent than in the events we know collectively as Holy Week and Easter. His audacious entry into Jerusalem and its Temple at Passover time was not what the city's entrenched religious leadership expected. Nor had His disciples expected Jesus to kneel and wash their feet, or to announce His betrayal, at what turned out to be their last supper together. His composure during His arrest, interrogation and trial confounded the powerful people—Jewish and Roman—who confronted Jesus, while His suffering and death on the Cross confounded His followers even more. And no one, it seems—whether friend or foe—expected Jesus to rise from the dead on that first Easter morning—no one except Jesus Himself.

And what all this means is not exactly what many people expect today.

꘎꘎

The Resurrection of Jesus is the *essential* fact in all the history of humanity. But it is also a *disputed* fact—and always has been. It confounds expectations, even now. From the very beginning, many who have heard the news of the Resurrection have not believed it. And—now as then—there are, among those who do not believe this central truth of the Gospel, some who would go farther. There are those who do not want the story told or heard *at all.* They want the Gospel of Jesus Christ to die, just as Jesus died.

And yet, the story lives because Jesus lives. And the story must be told—and retold—along with the other key events that surround the Resurrection and provide its proper context: The Triumphal Entry of Jesus into Jerusalem (Palm Sunday); His institution of the Lord's Supper or Holy Communion (Maundy Thursday); and His Crucifixion (Good Friday)...

...which raises the question: How do pastors continue to preach the heart of our faith—the Resurrection of Jesus Christ and the critical events that led up to it—with fresh perspective and appropriate power year after year after year?

※

"By the grace of God and the inspiration of the Holy Spirit" is the primary answer.

But perhaps the sermons in this volume may also be of some help. Perhaps something in the pages that follow will stimulate a thought, or set curiosity or creativity coursing in a different direction. Sometimes a sermon—sometimes just a sentence or phrase within a sermon—will open a door to a new vision or understanding for the preacher who reads it. I hope this may be the case for you, if you are entrusted with this sacred vocation.

※

Of course, you do not have to be preparing your own sermons to profit from the sermons provided here. This volume is not intended just for the clergy—or even just for Christians. The Good News of Jesus Christ—of which the Holy Week and Easter events are the climax *(though not the conclusion)*—is even more critical for those who have not yet believed in Him to hear. So be warned: you may find among the sermons here something that is not exactly what *you* expected.

And whether you are clergy, laity or currently outside the body of Christian believers, I offer you this collection, hoping you will find in reading what I found in preparing and preaching: the presence of God, giving gifts of grace.

☙❧

A few words of explanation about practical matters may be in order at this point. To begin with, the sermons in this volume may seem shorter than you might expect—some very noticeably so. In my defense, I note that all of them were "time constrained": they were preached either in services being broadcast on radio, or in services that were part of a tightly scheduled sequence of services on Sunday morning.

I further note that when I have listened to others preach, I have, on occasion, thought the sermon could have been a bit shorter. Rarely have I thought a sermon needed to be longer. I hope you will find these sermons "just about right" in length.

As in my previous volume of sermons, *O Come, Let God Adore Us*, I have chosen to ignore modern convention and capitalize nouns and pronouns referring to Father, Son or Holy Spirit (except in copyrighted biblical passages).

I used several different translations of the Bible in the preparation of the sermons (according to the particular pew Bible used in the chapel or church where the sermon was preached). I indicate below each sermon's title the specific version of the Bible I used in preparing that sermon.

It was my intention to provide the biblical text(s) before each sermon. However, it became necessary to reduce the amount of copyrighted biblical material in the book. As a result, where more than one sermon was drawn from the same passage, the text is provided only once (before the first sermon using it). In subsequent sermons from that passage, a page number is provided to indicate where the reading is to be found (even though the version may not be the same). I regret this inconvenience and any confusion you may experience as a result of it.

The footnotes throughout the book were added after the sermons were delivered. When scripture is actually quoted, references include the version. When I paraphrase or merely allude to something in scripture, no version is indicated. Where a scripture passage or phrase is italicized in the body of the sermon but not referenced, it is part of the sermon's text(s).

And, finally, I have provided several indices I hope you will find useful.

I acknowledge, but do not apologize for, the fact that you will find some repetition of ideas, and even phrasing, as you make your way through the sermons. Though I always tried to approach these great subjects fresh and new in study and composition, my mind, like most, does not forget everything placed there in the past. And, perhaps, repeating what is worthy of repetition is not a bad thing.

I also acknowledge with gratitude the proofreading help of my wife, Joanne, and my good friend, Wes May. They found a lot more of my mistakes than I did. Their efforts will make your reading experience more pleasant. Any flaws you *do* find are *my* fault, not theirs: I put all of them in the book in the first place.

I pray that whether you read these pages in preparation for preaching, or for your own inspiration and contemplation, God may bless you in the process, with understanding, amazement, joy and hope.

He is Risen!

Sermons

Mark 11:1-10 RSV

¹ And when they drew near to Jerusalem, to Beth'phage and Bethany, at the Mount of Olives, he sent two of his disciples, ² and said to them, "Go into the village opposite you, and immediately as you enter it you will find a colt tied, on which no one has ever sat; untie it and bring it. ³ If any one says to you, 'Why are you doing this?' say, 'The Lord has need of it and will send it back here immediately.'" ⁴ And they went away, and found a colt tied at the door out in the open street; and they untied it. ⁵ And those who stood there said to them, "What are you doing, untying the colt?" ⁶ And they told them what Jesus had said; and they let them go. ⁷ And they brought the colt to Jesus, and threw their garments on it; and he sat upon it. ⁸ And many spread their garments on the road, and others spread leafy branches which they had cut from the fields. ⁹ And those who went before and those who followed cried out, "Hosanna! Blessed is he who comes in the name of the Lord! ¹⁰ Blessed is the kingdom of our father David that is coming! Hosanna in the highest!"

1.

Not Exactly What They Expected

Mark 11:1-10 RSV

This is Palm Sunday and Jesus is headed for Jerusalem. It's no accident: He made up His mind to go to Jerusalem a long time ago. It may be that He was always supposed to make this trip to Jerusalem. He told His disciples He *had* to go to Jerusalem—and He told them why.[1] And He told them what they could expect when He got there.

They didn't like the idea very much,[2] but Jesus isn't the sort of guy you're going to talk out of something He's committed to.[3] He's Jesus. And they're His disciples. And so they're all headed for Jerusalem.

But Jesus isn't just headed for Jerusalem, of course. He's headed for Jerusalem *at Passover*. It's like going to Washington, D.C., for the Fourth of July: Don't expect to find a parking place.

People are coming to Jerusalem from all over the world. The crowds are enormous, and that's because Jerusalem at Passover really *is* like a Jewish Fourth of July celebration. Passover remembers when God reached into Egypt and broke the chains

---

[1] Matthew 16:21.
[2] Matthew 16:22.
[3] Matthew 16:23.

that held their Hebrew ancestors in bondage. God sent death to Pharaoh's house, a death that *passed over* the children of Israel, and set them free.[4]

Now, we get pretty excited today about celebrating our independence—and we still have it. It's an even bigger deal to commemorate it when you had it and then lost it. The Jewish people are not just focused on what it was like when they had their independence, they're looking for the chance to get it back from the Romans who rule over them—and for *somebody* who can make that happen.

So, there's Jesus and His disciples, and a hundred thousand patriotic pilgrims (give or take), all going to Jerusalem for Passover.

Some of these pilgrims have listened as Jesus talked to His disciples about the kingdom of God[5]—and they like what they've heard. Some of them have watched as Jesus talked that disgusting little Zacchaeus down out of a tree and into giving a fortune to the poor,[6] and then as Jesus lifted a pitiful, blind Bartimaeus up out of the dust and made him see.[7] And they're amazed by what *they've* seen. They don't know what Jesus knows about this trip to Jerusalem. They just think He would make a pretty good king.

And, why not? A lot of people who spend time with Jesus think the same thing. He's impressive. He isn't like other people. He isn't what you expect.

So, it's Passover time, and they're patriotic pilgrims, and there's Jerusalem, and they want a king.

Right time. Right place. Right man. Surely, He's the One! These people want Jesus to be their king.

---

[4] Exodus 12:29-32.
[5] Luke 18:16-17.
[6] Luke 19:1-10.
[7] Mark 10:46-52.

Luke says, *"As he was now drawing near, at the descent of the Mount of Olives, the whole multitude of the disciples began to rejoice and praise God with a loud voice for all the mighty works that they had seen."*[8]

They come to the Mount of Olives, with Jerusalem right in front of them, and they get all excited. And they get the disciples all excited. And before you know it, they're all singing and shouting and "testifying" and taking up an offering! (Well, maybe not that last part.) But they're marching into Jerusalem like their team just won the tournament to the tune of "Blessed is he who comes in the name of the Lord!"

"Yes sir! Now we're going to get some action! We got ourselves a king!"

⁓⁓

But there's a problem.

Not everybody is laying palm branches down in front of Jesus and singing "Hosanna!"

Yes, *these* people want Jesus to be king.

But there are also people who want just the opposite. There are people up there in Jerusalem who want Jesus dead.

Matthew says, *"…the chief priests and the elders of the people gathered in the palace of the high priest…and took counsel together in order to arrest Jesus by stealth and kill him."*[9]

These people—these very powerful and important people—are laying some very clever traps for Jesus on His way to whatever coronation the "king-makers" have in mind.

And Jesus doesn't seem to be helping the situation. He doesn't work very hard to avoid the traps. If anything, He goes out of His way to jump right in the middle of them.

The events that await Jesus are not at all what His enthusiastic fans expect when they start paving the Mount Olive road with their garments and greenery. Before long, they realize: He isn't following

---

[8] Luke 19:37, RSV.
[9] Matthew 26:3-4, RSV.

their game plan at all. How can Jesus be their king if He won't do things their way?

Jesus rides right into the stronghold of the enemy.

How is He going to escape capture?

He doesn't escape. Within a week, He surrenders without a struggle to the posse sent out to grab Him.[10]

How is He going to avoid conviction?

He doesn't avoid it. He offers no defense to their trumped-up charges against Him.[11]

And when the Roman governor in Jerusalem puts the question about kingship to Jesus point blank in the 18th Chapter of John, *"Are You the King of the Jews?"*[12]—all Jesus answers is that His kingdom is neither *of* this world nor *from* it.[13]

How is Jesus going to survive if His enemies decide to put Him to death?

He doesn't survive. Just five days after His triumphal entry into Jerusalem, Jesus is marched right back out again—but not to the Mount of Olives. This time He goes to another mount, one called "Golgotha." And there Jesus dies, to the cynical satisfaction of His enemies.[14]

It turns out that Jesus is not the kind of King Who drives the Romans out of Jewish territory; He drives the merchants and moneychangers out of the Jewish Temple.[15]

He doesn't rally an army of the faithful; He submits to an armed mob of His enemies.[16]

---

[10] John 18:1-8.
[11] Matthew 27:11-14.
[12] John 18:33, RSV.
[13] John 18:36, RSV.
[14] Matthew 27:35-43.
[15] Matthew 21:12.
[16] Matthew 26:47-54.

Why do these enemies want to kill Him? Why won't they accept Jesus as their king, the way the disciples and pilgrims do?

Well, the Pharisees in the group don't want Jesus to be their king because they're looking for somebody who is better behaved and shows more respect for law and tradition.[17]

The Sadducees don't want Jesus as their king because they prefer somebody with more sophistication and a greater appreciation for the nuances of power.[18]

And they both get what they want, it seems.

※

But His enemies have a problem, too. After all, if Jesus is not your king, who's left?

"We have no king but Caesar,"[19] they declare in John's Gospel.

If you don't take Jesus when He's offered, whom do you get?

"Give us Barabbas!"[20] they shout in Matthew's Gospel.

Caesar and Barabbas—there's a proud pair of consolation prizes for those who are determined that Jesus will not be their king! And if I may anticipate just a bit: Suppose, after all that, killing Jesus won't actually keep Him from being King, anyway?

※

By Friday, the enemies of Jesus will be jubilant. Not so, those who want Jesus to be their king. As it turns out, the Palm Sunday people can't make Him king.

Oh, they can stage a pep rally. They can march in a parade.

But despite all their enthusiasm, Jesus comes down off the donkey and goes up on the Cross and the "happy Hosannas" of that Palm Sunday's celebration are swallowed up in the gaping sinkhole of Good Friday's grief.

---

[17] Luke 6:1-11.
[18] John 11:47-50.
[19] John 19:15, RSV.
[20] Matthew 27:20-21, RSV.

Those who want Jesus to be king don't want Him to die. Those who want Jesus to die don't want Him to be king. Jesus says He is a King[21] and then He dies, willingly.[22] Both His supporters and His enemies get what they want—briefly—but neither group really gets what it expects. Both sides get it wrong.

"If we can just get Jesus to let us make Him a king, everything will be just like we want it to be."

"If we can just crucify Jesus, everything will be just like we want it to be."

Robert Burns, the Scottish poet, wrote:
>"The best-laid schemes
>o' mice an' men
>Gang aft agley."[23]

(Don't try to adjust your hearing aids. That's Scottish—or Celtic. The English equivalent is: "Go often askew.")

You see, one group wants to make Jesus a king. The other wants to make Him a corpse. And Jesus has come to be both. Jesus comes to Jerusalem as the King Who will die—because that is what *God* wants.

Jesus tells His disciples in Matthew that He *"came not to be served, but to serve, and to give his life a ransom for many."*[24]

God sends a King to pay a King's ransom for people God judges worth the expense.[25] Robbie Burns may be right about the plans of mice and men, but the same doesn't apply to the plans of God. Things in Jerusalem go exactly according to *God's* plan. It is *exactly* what God expected.

And if that doesn't make sense, consider an explanation of this mystery from God in Isaiah:

---

[21] John 18:36-37.
[22] John 10:17-18.
[23] Robert Burns, "Tae a Moose (English: "To a Mouse"), on Turning Her Up in Her Nest with the Plough," *Poems, Chiefly in the Scottish Dialect,* Kilmarnock, Scotland: John Wilson, 1785.
[24] Matthew 20:28, RSV.
[25] John 3:16.

> *"...my thoughts are not your thoughts,*
> *neither are your ways my ways, says the* LORD.
> *For as the heavens are higher than the earth,*
> *so are my ways higher than your ways*
> *and my thoughts than your thoughts....*
> *so shall my word be that goes forth from my mouth;*
> *it shall not return to me empty,*
> *but it shall accomplish that which I purpose,*
> *and prosper in the thing for which I sent it."*[26]

And remember that John says that Jesus is the Word made flesh Who dwelt among us.[27] Even now, the supporters of Jesus can't control Him and His enemies can't get rid of Him. He's still doing what God wants, and He always will. You might as well get used to it.

Let's make it personal: What do you expect of Jesus? Do you expect Him to be your King? And if so, what do you expect your King to do? Jesus did what a king does for his people: He saved them.[28] And even now, Jesus is still doing for His people what a king does: He's ruling over us.[29]

Isaac Watts' hymn says it pretty well:
> "Jesus shall reign where e'er the sun
> Does his successive journeys run.
> His kingdom spread from shore to shore
> Till moons shall wax and wane no more."[30]

Jesus is your King, but He won't do things your way. How many times do you pray for one thing and get something else? How many times do you hope for the easy way and get the hard way instead? If you make Jesus your King, why doesn't He just "get with the (*your*) program"?

---

[26] Isaiah 55:8, 9 and 11, RSV.
[27] John 1:14.
[28] Romans 5:6-10.
[29] Revelation 11:15.
[30] Isaac Watts, "Jesus Shall Reign Where E'er the Sun," *The Psalms of David*, 1719.

The truth is that you cannot "make" Jesus your King any more than the Passover pilgrims in Jerusalem could. But you can acknowledge that *God* has made Him your King.

In the same way, you cannot prevent Jesus from being your King any more than His enemies in Jerusalem could. But you can live in rebellion against His sovereignty and incur the judgment such rebellion deserves.

When it comes to kings, we Americans just don't get it. We've been raised all our lives with "of the people, by the people, and for the people."[31] We may not be able to quote it, but we certainly assume the truth of the assertion in the Declaration of Independence that "...governments are instituted among men, deriving their just powers from the consent of the governed."[32] We think we ought to have a "say" in who's in charge. That's fine for human society, but it's a problem for our relationship with God.

God has appointed Jesus King. And you need to understand that Jesus is the kind of King that Paul describes when he says *"that at the name of Jesus every knee shall bow...and every tongue confess that Jesus Christ is Lord...."*[33]

Crown Him or crucify Him, Jesus is still going to be the King God has appointed Him to be. If you don't understand Him, that may be why. If you can't control Him, that may be why. If you can't get rid of Him, that may be why as well.

You might as well just brush up on your "Hosanna!" singing, because Jesus *is* the King Who comes in the Name of the Lord.

---

[31] Abraham Lincoln, *The Gettysburg Address*, Gettysburg, Pennsylvania, November 19, 1863.
[32] Thomas Jefferson, *The Declaration of Independence*, Philadelphia, Pennsylvania, July 4, 1776.
[33] Philippians 2:10-11, RSV.

Palm Sunday

2 Samuel 5:1-3, 6-7 ESV

¹ Then all the tribes of Israel came to David at Hebron and said, "Behold, we are your bone and flesh. ² In times past, when Saul was king over us, it was you who led out and brought in Israel. And the LORD said to you, 'You shall be shepherd of my people Israel, and you shall be prince over Israel.'" ³ So all the elders of Israel came to the king at Hebron, and King David made a covenant with them at Hebron before the LORD, and they anointed David king over Israel.

⁶ And the king and his men went to Jerusalem against the Jebusites, the inhabitants of the land, who said to David, "You will not come in here, but the blind and the lame will ward you off"—thinking, "David cannot come in here." ⁷ Nevertheless, David took the stronghold of Zion, that is, the city of David.

They Could Not Keep Him Out

John 12:12-16 ESV

[12] The next day the large crowd that had come to the feast heard that Jesus was coming to Jerusalem. [13] So they took branches of palm trees and went out to meet him, crying out, "Hosanna! Blessed is he who comes in the name of the Lord, even the King of Israel!" [14] And Jesus found a young donkey and sat on it, just as it is written,

> [15] "Fear not, daughter of Zion;
> behold, your king is coming,
> sitting on a donkey's colt!"

[16] His disciples did not understand these things at first, but when Jesus was glorified, then they remembered that these things had been written about him and had been done to him.

2.

They Could Not Keep Him Out

2 Samuel 5:1-3, 6-7; John 12:12-16 ESV

Today, we wave the palms and sing "Hosanna!" to commemorate the Triumphal Entry of Jesus into Jerusalem, the holy city of God. But before you settle in to enjoy the parade, you may want to take another look. The gospel writers make it sound like "a good time was had by all." Or, at least, that's the way we read it, because that's what it's become for us.

But things aren't always what they seem (especially in the Gospel of John), and a closer look may reveal some significant problems with the pageant about to proceed up the hill.

The word is out that Jesus is coming to Jerusalem. He's been on His way for some time; it's been no secret. Jesus has been making His way very methodically through the Holy Land to arrive at the gates of the holy city amid the multitude of Passover pilgrims. And He's been performing miracles along the way, just to make the journey interesting: a blind man healed here,[34] a dead person raised there.[35] Jesus has made a name for Himself—and they've certainly heard of Him in Jerusalem.

---

[34] Mark 10:46-52.
[35] John 11:38-44.

They Could Not Keep Him Out

But the people making all the fuss over Jesus as He approaches are not the fine citizens of this sacred city. There's no dignified delegation of the City Council or Chamber of Commerce—or even the local Clergy Club—marching out to meet Him. The *"large crowd"* John describes are the "out-of-towners"—other pilgrims. Luke[36] says "the multitude" is *"the whole multitude **of His disciples**."* Matthew[37] and Mark[38] talk about *"many,"* and *"most of the crowd"* and *"others"*—leaving the actual count rather vague.

And Jesus is left to secure His own transportation, which He does by sending His disciples to commandeer a donkey from the pool of pack animals most villages keep available in the square, specifically for that purpose.[39] Jesus mounts the beast and the scene begins to look for all the world like a royal arrival at the gates. Jesus mounts a donkey, just like King Solomon did[40]—and probably his father David before him—a thousand years before Jesus—to come into their kingdom—and arrive at their throne—in Jerusalem.

The disciples of Jesus, and at least some of the other pilgrims, "strike up the band" (metaphorically speaking). He looks like the King to them. All Jesus needs is for the Official Welcoming Committee to come out of Jerusalem and offer the standard honors that any arriving dignitary is due.

But the committee never comes. They never come out.

So Jesus comes in.

Despite their insult—despite the opposition and hostility that are so obvious in their action (or lack of it)—the good and great citizens of the City of God cannot keep God's Messiah—the

---

[36] Luke 19:37-38, ESV.
[37] Matthew 21:8-9, ESV.
[38] Mark 11:8-9, ESV.
[39] See J. Duncan M. Derrett, "Law in the New Testament: The Palm Sunday Colt," *Novum Testamentum*, Vol. 13, Fasc. 4 (October 1971), pp. 241-258.
[40] 1 Kings 1:32-40.

rightful and coming King—out. He rides right up to the Temple and enters the place where priests and people proclaim the Presence of God to dwell.[41]

But they don't want *Jesus* there—these professionals who perform their duties as the holy smoke rises to heaven every day. They don't want Him there—even though He is the Presence of God Who came down from heaven in human form[42] and is now face to face with them. They don't want Jesus there because they sense He's about to turn everything they stand for on its head. He's about to cast everything out of the Temple they have gladly brought into it[43]—while *they* try to figure out a politically safe way to throw *Him* out of the Temple[44]—and out of this world.[45]

And they *will* figure it out, of course—in just a few days. They will see to it that this One, Who rode into town like a King borne upon a donkey and propelled by the praise of the pilgrims, will go out, burdened like a criminal under a cross[46] and assaulted by the insults of those who arranged His execution.[47] And they will be so satisfied with themselves and what they've accomplished—or *think* they have accomplished…

…until they discover that—even when they kill Him—they cannot keep Him out.

త్రోత్ర

When King David first came to Jerusalem to make it his capital—the place where he would rule—his enemies were sure they could keep *him* out—out of what they considered their impregnable domain.

---

[41] Mark 11:11.
[42] Philippians 2:6-7.
[43] Matthew 21:12-13.
[44] Luke 19:47-48.
[45] Matthew 26:3-5.
[46] John 19:16-18.
[47] Matthew 27:41-43.

"The blind and the lame will ward you off, Davie Boy!" they jeered. "You'll never get to us—never get past our defenses—never come where we are."

And then, in a way and with a speed they had never imagined, David was "there" and the city was his. He had overcome all their defenses—and he was their king.

☙❧

And in the same way, the leaders of a later Jerusalem raised their defenses—they ridiculed the Prince of Peace, the Messiah of God, coming to them in accordance with the ancient promises[48]—humble and riding on a donkey. If they thought the blind and the lame could keep Jesus out of Jerusalem, they were just as mistaken as their ancient ancestors were about *His* ancestor, David. Jesus made the blind to see and the lame to walk.[49] Why would *they* want to keep Him out?

It seemed so simple to ignore Him. And when that didn't work, it seemed as though it would be embarrassingly easy to "eliminate" Him. Trump up some charges.[50] Manipulate the Roman magistrate.[51] Torture this Jesus to near madness.[52] And then hang Him on a cross and watch His life slowly drain away.[53]

But alive or dead, they could not keep Him out. On Palm Sunday, Jesus came triumphantly through the great open gates of the city. A week later, He came even more triumphantly through the small, locked door of a room of no importance in the city,[54] except that the room was filled with His disciples, who thought He could not come in—there or anywhere—because He was dead.

But He did come in.

---

[48] Zechariah 9:9-10.
[49] Matthew 15:30-31.
[50] Mark 14:55-59.
[51] John 19:12-16.
[52] John 19:1-3.
[53] Mark 15:25, 33-37.
[54] John 20:19.

They could not keep Him out—and they didn't try. Jesus, the Teacher from Galilee—Who entered Jerusalem with all the symbolism of a king—*was* a king—*is* a king—is THE King—is *their* King. He is the King no one can keep out.

Oh, there are many who want to—and try to—keep Him out, still.

"I don't believe in Jesus. I don't want any part of Him. Don't bother me with your 'holy hogwash'—your religious rituals and routine. You can't force me to listen, and you couldn't convince me if I did. You can't get through to me with Jesus. My defenses are too strong. He's not my King and He's not coming into my life."

And if that's the way you're thinking, you're wrong—simply—dangerously—wrong.

Yes, you can put up your defenses. You can ignore our entreaties and those of the Holy Spirit. You can reject our arguments and those of the Bible. You can put every barrier possible between you and the Jesus Who wants to—and has a right to—rule over you.

Many people do. And they hold Him off year after year after year. And that, they can do—*you* can do—because, like the words of Revelation[55] say, Jesus stands at the door and knocks—just knocks, politely—and calls, of course, but lovingly. And if you hear His voice and open the door, He will come in to you—and share the goodness of God with you.

☙◦❧

And if you do *not* invite Him in, He will *not* come in—though He could. Instead, He will wait. He never goes away, though you may think He has. You see, Jesus is patient as well as polite. And He is the King—your King—whether you acknowledge Him or not. Jesus is the King Who has the right to rule over you. And He

---

[55] Revelation 3:20.

can afford to be patient because He knows that He *will* reign over you—by your voluntary submission in this life—or without it, in the next.

Paul put it this way: *"...at the name of Jesus, every knee should bow, in heaven and on earth and under the earth* (which pretty much covers all the categories available)—*and every tongue confess that Jesus Christ is Lord."*[56]

And when will that be?

When you are no longer in a position to keep Him out—and He is no longer willing to let you—and when you are no longer in a position to benefit from letting Him in.

When will that be?

When you go out of this world—as you will one day—or He comes back into it, as *He* will one day.

John put it this way in the Book of Revelation: *"Then the seventh angel blew his trumpet, and there were loud voices in heaven, saying, 'The kingdom of the world has become the kingdom of our Lord and of his Christ, and he shall reign forever and ever!'"*[57]

❧

Here's the funny thing: *"The kingdom of this world"* has *always* been *"the kingdom of our Lord and of His Christ,"* from the first instant in time when He created it. He has always been the only rightful King of this kingdom in which we are all subjects, whether rebellious or faithful. And He will always be the only rightful King of this kingdom, forever and ever, Amen.

So, what's the point of pretending otherwise? What's the point of "passing" on His parade? What's the point of putting up the barricades and trying to keep Jesus out of your life when all you're really doing is delaying your inevitable submission and diminishing the joy and wonder that comes with joining the royal procession

---

[56] Philippians 2:10-11, ESV.
[57] Revelation 11:15, ESV.

Palm Sunday

and making the most of His triumphal entry into your heart—that place where He has the right to rule anyway?

What's the point?

There isn't any point.

They could not keep Jesus out of Jerusalem any more than David could be kept out a thousand years before. And you cannot keep Jesus out. Nor should you.

You can ignore Him. You can attack Him. But it won't keep Him from being the King Who will, sooner or later, rule over everybody everywhere, including you.

And if you make Him your King now?

You get to march in His royal parade. You get to go out to meet Him and welcome Him and usher Him into your life. You get to celebrate His arrival. You get to go to heaven with Him and enjoy His blessings on earth.

And if Revelation is to be believed, you get to sit with Him on His throne in heaven,[58] which, you'll admit, not a lot of other kings would ever let you do.

When the leaders of Israel went to make David their king, they told him, "You led us out and brought us in." They said, "God made you His shepherd over us to rule over us."

And so, we say to David's greatest descendant, Jesus: "Be our King. Lead us. Shepherd us. Come and rule over us. You are the King."

---

[58] Revelation 3:21.

Zechariah 9:9-10 ESV

⁹ Rejoice greatly, O daughter of Zion!
　Shout aloud, O daughter of Jerusalem!
Behold, your king is coming to you;
　righteous and having salvation is he,
humble and mounted on a donkey,
　on a colt, the foal of a donkey.
10 I will cut off the chariot from Ephraim
　and the war horse from Jerusalem;
and the battle bow shall be cut off,
　and he shall speak peace to the nations;
his rule shall be from sea to sea,
　and from the River to the ends of the earth.

Look Who's Here

Matthew 21:1-11 ESV

¹ *Now when they drew near to Jerusalem and came to Bethphage, to the Mount of Olives, then Jesus sent two disciples,* ² *saying to them, "Go into the village in front of you, and immediately you will find a donkey tied, and a colt with her. Untie them and bring them to me.* ³ *If anyone says anything to you, you shall say, 'The Lord needs them,' and he will send them at once."* ⁴ *This took place to fulfill what was spoken by the prophet, saying,*

> ⁵ *"Say to the daughter of Zion,*
> *'Behold, your king is coming to you,*
> *humble, and mounted on a donkey,*
> *on a colt, the foal of a beast of burden.'"*

⁶ *The disciples went and did as Jesus had directed them.* ⁷ *They brought the donkey and the colt and put on them their cloaks, and he sat on them.* ⁸ *Most of the crowd spread their cloaks on the road, and others cut branches from the trees and spread them on the road.* ⁹ *And the crowds that went before him and that followed him were shouting, "Hosanna to the Son of David! Blessed is he who comes in the name of the Lord! Hosanna in the highest!"* ¹⁰ *And when he entered Jerusalem, the whole city was stirred up, saying, "Who is this?"* ¹¹ *And the crowds said, "This is the prophet Jesus, from Nazareth of Galilee."*

3.

Look Who's Here

Zechariah 9:9-10; Matthew 21:1-11 ESV

Did you know that in everything that happens, there is a message from God—or a revelation about God—or a gift of God—to anyone with eyes to see it or faith to receive it? God is at work in all things—in all *good* things to bless—and in all *bad* things to redeem.[59] God is in your favorite song and a perfect spring day and hugs at church to insert a bit of the divine in your life. At the same time, God is in evil, so that it does not completely overwhelm you—and in pain, so that it is not purposeless—and in death, so that its loss is not final.

Many people would respond (and you may be one of them): "*I* don't see God in the things that are happening to me. I don't see God in *most* of the things happening in the world."

But are you looking?

☙❧

Recently, I was waiting to lead a group of ladies in a special service of comfort and encouragement. Most of the members of

---

[59] Romans 8:28.

the group are not members of our congregation, but they are loved and supported by many who are.

As the time for the meeting drew near, several of our members got up from their seats and went to the windows to look out—to look for specific individuals they expected to see. They wanted them to come, and their desire to see them led them to focus their attention on the way to where we were. And because they were looking, the time came when they saw those they were looking for, and so were ready to greet them, with joy and affection, when they arrived.

God comes to us in every aspect of our lives—good and bad—great and small—in the out of the ordinary occurrences as well as the familiar routine. *"Lo, I am with you always."*[60]

But are you looking?

※

You know, if you could boil all the inspired words of the Bible down to one, it might just be: "Look!" The Bible from start to finish tells about the God Who created everything—and has been interacting with everything—in an attempt to get the crown of His Creation (us) to see Him and Who He is and how He wants to relate to us. In the Garden of Eden, God came looking for the people He lovingly created.[61] And ever since, God has been trying to get our attention—to get us to look at Him, or, at least, to look *for* Him, around us and within us.

But so often, we don't. We don't look for—and so we don't see—God.

The Russian author Leo Tolstoy wrote a lovely and well-known story about a simple cobbler—an old man with no family—who, late one night, somewhere between waking and sleeping, heard a voice he took to be Jesus, telling him, "Look out into the street tomorrow, for I shall come."

---

[60] Matthew 28:20, RSV.
[61] Genesis 3:8-9.

And all the next day—from early morning till night—he looked out his window, waiting for his Lord to come. And throughout the day, the cobbler saw many people, some of whom needed help, which he gave. But Jesus, he did not see.

That night, he heard the Voice again, calling him by name: "Martin, don't you know Me?" But what he saw was face after face of the people he had helped.

The cobbler had been looking for God and had seen God without knowing it. The title of the story? "Where Love is, There God is Also."[62]

Here was a man who saw God out his window all day long, even though he didn't recognize Him. But he *did* see God, because he was looking.

But what do the little cobbler—or the ladies looking out the windows of our church, for that matter—have to do with the Triumphal Entry of Jesus into Jerusalem we read about in Matthew's gospel?

The link is that the Jews had been looking for someone, too. Not for a few minutes or a day, but for years and years—for centuries. A whole people—generation after generation—had been looking for God.

They had been told in sacred scripture that God's Messiah would come,[63] and they wanted God's Messiah to come because they had been promised that God would come in him—or with him, at least—to empower the Messiah and guide him and give him success in delivering God's people from a life in which they could not see God or believe Him present with them.[64]

---

[62] Leo Tolstoy, "Where Love Is, There God Is Also," 1895, translated by Nathan Haskell Dole, in the Crowell Company's *Worth While Booklet Series*.
[63] Isaiah 11.
[64] Jeremiah 23:5-8.

But though they were looking for God's Messiah, the story of the Bible is that they did not recognize Him when He came.[65] So many people could not see Who Jesus was.

〜

The same is true today.

In the Gospel reading, Jesus was making a name for Himself—to the degree that it was possible for anybody to make a name for himself in a time before the 24-hour news cycle and social media. But even those who saw Jesus didn't recognize Him for Who He was. Even those who were willing to give up their garments to make a saddle for Jesus to sit on, or a carpet for His donkey to walk on, couldn't see Who they were really dealing with.

"Who is it?"

"It's Jesus, the prophet from Nazareth."

True, in one sense, but so inadequate.

"Jesus?"

Yes, and Christ—and Savior—and Lord.[66]

"From Nazareth?"

Yes, and before that, from heaven—from the right hand of God the Father Almighty, in fact.[67]

"Prophet?"

Yes, in that He spoke the word of God. But He was, and is, also, the eternal Word of God and only-begotten Son of God.[68]

〜

You've got to look for Him to see Him, but you have to know Who you're looking at when you do see Him, which you will, because He's there. Everywhere. All the time.

---

[65] John 1:9-11.
[66] Luke 2:11.
[67] Philippians 2:6.
[68] John 1:1-3; 3:16.

Look for God in everything. Look! He's there—in everything—blessing or redeeming.

And as you look, know Who it is you're looking for—and at. Not "nice-guy Jesus." Not "good-example Jesus." Not "maybe-a-prophet-from-Nazareth Jesus." Certainly not "dress-Him-up-to-look-just-like-you-want-Him-to-look Jesus."

Know that you're looking for and at *"the Lamb of God, Who takes away the sin of the world"*[69] Jesus. You're looking at the *"King of kings and Lord of lords"*[70] Jesus. You're looking at the *"I will never leave you nor forsake you"*[71] Jesus and the *"I have overcome the world"*[72] (for you) Jesus. That's Who He is. That's His message—His revelation—His gift to you—in everything.

❧

But we're not done.

Look—Who's—*here*.

They were looking "out there" for the Messiah. They were looking "out there" for God. They were looking for Him on battlefields and in royal throne rooms and atop the Temple's towers. They were looking "there."

And God came "here"—as a baby born in a stable to be raised in a backwater village. He came "here"—into manhood and His ministry—without academic awards—without political position or patronage—without military might. He showed up one day with a bunch of pilgrims, plodding up a dusty road, and when He could see His destination, He got on a borrowed donkey and rode it into town. And the people looking for God "out there" turned around to find Him "here"—with them.

Look—Who's—*here*.

Yes, God is "there." As the song says,

---

[69] John 1:29, ESV.
[70] Revelation 19:16, ESV.
[71] Hebrews 13:5, ESV.
[72] John 16:33, ESV.

"I see the stars.
I hear the rolling thunder.
Thy power throughout
the universe displayed."[73]

God is "there"—everywhere. But more importantly—for each of us—God is "here."

It's the Gospel. It's what the angels told the shepherds outside Bethlehem: *"unto you is born this day… a Savior, Christ the Lord,"*[74]—and what Andrew told Peter when he first met Jesus: *"We have found the Messiah."*[75] And He is "here"—with us.

Look—Who's—*here*.

❧

"Where two or three are gathered in my name," Jesus said, *"there am I among them."*[76] God is here with you—today—in *this* place. God is here—today—with you in this church building because, in reality, *we* are the church and wherever *we* are, God is "here" with us. God is "here" in the atrium when we gather together, and in the classrooms when we study together, and in the fellowship hall when we eat together, and in the conference room when we meet to work on projects together, and when we visit together in our homes and go shopping or play golf together.

And God is "here" with us in the secret places of our hearts when we pray in private and read our Bibles and struggle with our sorrows and worry about our loved ones—and the world in general—and respond to the daily demands of our lives. And God will be "here" with us when we leave this world for the final, truly permanent and all-glorious home that awaits us all when *we* are no longer "here."

---

[73] Carl Gustav Boberg, "How Great Thou Art," 1885. The hymn was translated into English from the Russian by English missionary Stuart K. Hine, who also added two additional verses of his own.
[74] Luke 2:11, KJV.
[75] John 1:40-41, ESV.
[76] Matthew 18:20, ESV.

Wherever "here" is for a Christian, that is where God is. Yes, God is also "out there," speaking, showing, revealing His nature and His will in everything we see and experience in our world. But what you see, discover and learn from God about God "out there" is all for the purpose of knowing the God Who is "here," with you and within you, blessing and redeeming your life.

All things are not God, but God created all things[77] and is at work in all things.[78] Look for Him "there."

Everybody has an idea of Who they want God to be. See Him for Who He really is. You can see God "there" in the world. But know that He is "here"— with us—with *you*.

Look—Who's—here.

---

[77] John 1:1-2.
[78] Romans 8:28.

Maundy Thursday

A Meal to Remember

Luke 22:7-8, 13-20 ESV

⁷ Then came the day of Unleavened Bread, on which the Passover lamb had to be sacrificed. ⁸ So Jesus sent Peter and John, saying, "Go and prepare the Passover for us, that we may eat it."

¹³ And they went and found it just as he had told them, and they prepared the Passover.

¹⁴ And when the hour came, he reclined at table, and the apostles with him. ¹⁵ And he said to them, "I have earnestly desired to eat this Passover with you before I suffer. ¹⁶ For I tell you I will not eat it until it is fulfilled in the kingdom of God." ¹⁷ And he took a cup, and when he had given thanks he said, "Take this, and divide it among yourselves. ¹⁸ For I tell you that from now on I will not drink of the fruit of the vine until the kingdom of God comes." ¹⁹ And he took bread, and when he had given thanks, he broke it and gave it to them, saying, "This is my body, which is given for you. Do this in remembrance of me." ²⁰ And likewise the cup after they had eaten, saying, "This cup that is poured out for you is the new covenant in my blood."

4.

A Meal to Remember

Luke 22:7-8, 13-20 ESV

My next-door neighbor is dying. The doctors give him six months; his wife says he will go much sooner. He is a genuine hero, with a Silver Star to prove it. He served with courage and distinction in combat, and then taught others to do the same.

One day this week, many of these people, his closest friends, came to his house for a picnic—to share one last meal with the man who taught them so much—the man they came to love. Sharing this meal with them meant so much to my neighbor. And they, in turn, will remember him—and this one last meal they had with him—for the rest of their lives.

☙❦

According to the scripture we just read, Jesus of Nazareth is dying, as sure as my next-door neighbor. It isn't cancer that will do Jesus in. He will die of acute crucifixion—being nailed to a cross. And it won't be in six months, but any day, maybe even tomorrow.

And yet, maybe He *will* die of cancer, in a way—the cancer of sin, which kills everybody in the end, and will kill Him—not because He *has* it—which He doesn't—but because everybody else does.[79] And by dying *for* them—dying with *their* cancer—He can cure them—everybody—of the cancer of sin—by killing sin as it kills Him. But let's leave that for another day.

                         ⁂

On the night before He dies, His closest friends share a special, last meal with Jesus. It is no picnic—no party. They all sense that He could die any day—and that they might die with Him. It is no picnic at all.

It is, however—appropriately—a *Passover* dinner, a reminder of a time when death was all around and deliverance came out of the terrifying darkness.[80] They eat the meal together before the beginning of Passover because, this year, Passover will once again bring deliverance through death—the death of Jesus.

But this meal—like the Passover meal—is for remembering. Jesus had called these people gathered in this room with Him to a special life—a special relationship with Him. Day after day, He had taught them, shown them wonders of wisdom and power, destroyed their assumptions about life and God and themselves, and replaced those assumptions with remarkable revelations of truth and grace and love. Then He sent them out to repeat the wonders and reveal the truth to others—which they did, with ever-increasing confidence and effect.

But just when they are ready to celebrate what He has enabled them to achieve, He tells them He is going to die.[81] Their first reaction is denial, of course, and then anger, which is also normal. They are confused. Their confidence is shaken. Fear and depression set in.

What are they going to do if the One Who has taught them everything goes away? How will they live without the One Who

---

[79] 2 Corinthians 5:21.
[80] Exodus 11 and 12.
[81] Matthew 16:21-23.

has enabled them—empowered them—to live in this wonderful new way?

And if *they* are concerned about *themselves* at the prospect of losing Jesus, Jesus is concerned about them, too. He knows that His death is not the end for them; it is just the beginning.

But He also knows that they don't know this—that they can't understand how this could be so.

And so, He must teach them even this: that in His death, there is life for them. And to teach them this last, great lesson, Jesus takes His disciples to dinner. And in this last meal before He dies, He makes them see what it all means—He provides them the means to remember.

ॐ

First, Jesus takes the bread on the table, and like any good Jew (and even most bad ones), He says grace before breaking it. And He gives them pieces—pieces of bread. And He tells them, "This bread is My Body, which is broken—for you. As often as you do this, do it in remembrance of Me."

As often as you hold a communion service?

"No, as often as you sit down to eat a meal, remember *this* meal. As often as you put bread on the table, remember *this* bread and what I say it means. And as often as you take something as simple and basic as bread in your hands to bless it and break it and eat it, remember that My Body will be given into the hands of those who will curse It and consume It in hatred, even though God has blessed It in love to feed you with life eternal.

"Every time you sit down to a meal, remember. Every time you put food in your mouth, remember. Even if all you have is a crust of bread, remember that I am the Bread of life and have fed you—and feed you still."

"This is My Body," He told them, "Which is broken for you. Remember."

And then, the cup. The wine in the cup encourages remembering. Red like blood—life's blood—wine can be spilled. Accidents happen. But in this case, His Blood—His sacred Blood—will be poured out like wine, not by accident, but intentionally and voluntarily, as a priceless, sacrificial offering.

But before that, wine like His Blood will be shared with them, just as Jesus has shared His life with them.

"The wine in this cup is My Blood that will be poured out for you. But first, this wine will be given *to* you—as the source and sustaining power of everlasting life has been. As often as you drink it, remember."

As often as you dip your bread or host in the chalice at communion? As often as you sip the contents of the communion cup?

"No, as often you take a cup or glass or goblet in your hand and raise it to your mouth to drink. Every time you take a sip of wine, or water, or whatever drink you drink to relieve your thirst or just 'wet your whistle'—remember."

Remember that Jesus is What we all ultimately thirst for. Remember that when there was nothing to satisfy the emptiness inside, Jesus came to meet that need at the cost of His own life, with the shedding of His own Blood. Remember, not just on Maundy Thursday or Communion Sunday, but every time you take a bite or sip of anything.

☙❧

Remember, every time you take a breath, in fact, because the very air you breathe is His gift, and an every-moment reminder of His promise to sustain your life, for a little longer, at least, in this world, and forever in the next, through His saving, sacrificial grace.

His disciples—His friends—never forgot that meal—that last meal they shared with Him before He died. They never forgot, mainly, because He didn't stay dead. They remembered all He taught them—at that meal and throughout their time with Him—

Maundy Thursday

because He was raised from the dead and sent His Holy Spirit to *commune* with them—at all times and for all time—when He ascended into heaven.

And they repeated that meal, over and over and over again—to remind themselves of that first last supper—and to remind all those who became disciples and friends of Jesus after that meal of remembrance that these are now their memories, too—that each time any of the disciples of Jesus gather as He gathered His first disciples, Jesus gathers with them—with us—to help us remember—as we take the bread and the cup—what He did for us, and *is* doing for us, and *will* do for us, forever and ever, Amen.

Remember?

Delivery Charges

Exodus 12:21-32 RSV

²¹ Then Moses summoned all the elders of Israel and said to them, "Go at once and select the animals for your families and slaughter the Passover lamb.

²² "Take a bunch of hyssop, dip it into the blood in the basin and put some of the blood on the top and on both sides of the doorframe. Not one of you shall go out the door of his house until morning. ²³ When the LORD goes through the land to strike down the Egyptians, he will see the blood on the top and sides of the doorframe and will pass over that doorway, and he will not permit the destroyer to enter your houses and strike you down.

²⁴ "Obey these instructions as a lasting ordinance for you and your descendants. ²⁵ When you enter the land that the LORD will give you as he promised, observe this ceremony.

²⁶ "And when your children ask you, 'What does this ceremony mean to you?' ²⁷ then tell them, 'It is the Passover sacrifice to the LORD, who passed over the houses of the Israelites in Egypt and spared our homes when he struck down the Egyptians.'" Then the people bowed down and worshiped. ²⁸ The Israelites did just what the LORD commanded Moses and Aaron.

²⁹ At midnight the LORD struck down all the firstborn in Egypt, from the firstborn of Pharaoh, who sat on the throne, to the firstborn of the prisoner, who was in the dungeon, and the firstborn of all the livestock as well. ³⁰ Pharaoh and all his officials and all the Egyptians got up during the night, and there was loud wailing in Egypt, for there was not a house without someone dead.

³¹ During the night Pharaoh summoned Moses and Aaron and said, "Up! Leave my people, you and the Israelites! Go, worship the LORD as you have requested. ³² Take your flocks and herds, as you have said, and go...."

5.

Delivery Charges

Exodus 12:21-32; Luke 22:7-8, 13-20 RSV (p. 34)

Today, we enter the realm of ceremonies, customs, and traditions. Anyone associated with the military will be well-versed in such things, or at least better-versed than most without that connection.[82] But not all ceremonies take place on the parade field or the quarterdeck. Not all customs derive from the age of sail or knights on horseback. Some traditions are not military at all.

Today, we take part in a ceremony that takes place in Christian worship sites, both humble and sublime, around the world. The custom of Communion is one that all Christians hold dear, and repeat—some every month, some every week, some every day. The tradition goes back to Jesus Christ Himself, as the gospels and Paul[83] make clear. Listen to what Luke says in Chapter 22, verses 19 and 20: *"And he took bread, gave thanks and broke it, and gave it to them, saying, 'This is my body given for you; do this in remembrance of me.' In the same way, after the supper he took the cup, saying, 'This cup is the new covenant in my blood, which is poured out for you.'"*

---

[82] This sermon was preached in a Navy chapel where those present each week were overwhelmingly active duty or retired servicemembers.
[83] 1 Corinthians 11:23-25.

This is the heart of our Communion tradition: Jesus providing us a memorial ceremony. But this tradition is based on an older one still. Jesus was Himself participating in a well-known and time-honored ceremony when He established ours. This was no ordinary night on which Jesus offered His disciples the bread and cup. Jesus did not speak these words "out of the blue." Earlier in Chapter 22, Luke writes: *"Then came the day of Unleavened Bread on which the Passover lamb had to be sacrificed. Jesus sent Peter and John, saying, 'Go and make preparations for us to eat the Passover.'"*

❦

The ceremony that evening was part of the Passover process. The tradition was God's deliverance of His people from bondage in Egypt. And to understand the meaning of the Passover, we have to go back (as Jesus and His disciples did) to Exodus, Chapter 12. There God delivered His chosen people—the children of Israel—from a captivity imposed and enforced by Pharaoh, the king of Egypt. And just as with our military moves, the captives did not pay the cost of their deliverance from bondage any more than we pay for the delivery of our goods from our previous addresses.

But this doesn't mean that delivery—or deliverance—is free. In our case, the government pays the cost of delivering our household goods to us. We could not afford to move ourselves from one duty station to another every few years—and the captives didn't have the means to buy or bust their way out of captivity, even after 400 years.

But they *were* delivered.

So who paid for their deliverance? Their deliverance cost the lives of the Passover lamb and Pharaoh's firstborn son. That's who paid. But each died for a different reason in the plan for deliverance.

The death of the lamb provided the blood that protected God's people from the fatal power of the supernatural Destroyer unleashed by a God determined to deliver His chosen people from their bondage.

The death of Pharaoh's firstborn son was necessary to break the will of the earthly power that held God's people in bondage against *God's* will—a power determined to prevent their being delivered from bondage. To deliver the Hebrews from bondage in Egypt, God directed *them* to take the life of the Passover lamb, while *God* took the life of Pharaoh's son.

༄༅

This raises an important, but often overlooked, question: Did God *want* to take the life of Pharaoh's son?

It may have looked that way from the vantage point of the Hebrew captives. Certainly, they had been given no reason to care what happened to *any* of the Egyptians. No death—except perhaps that of Pharaoh himself—would have brought them greater satisfaction than that of the eldest son and heir of their ultimate tormentor!

To hear their God threaten Pharaoh with the death of his son if Pharaoh did not release the Hebrews from his control—and then to see their God carry out that threat to its fullest extent when Pharaoh rejected God's demand—would seem to captives waiting and praying for deliverance from Pharaoh an act so "right" that the very possibility of regret would be out of the question.

And yet...

༄༅

In the centuries that followed this final plague and first Passover, prophets like Isaiah came to understand that God's Lordship extends over *all* the nations.[84] Jonah was sent to demonstrate that Israel's God desires their enemies' *conversion*, not destruction.[85]

---

[84] Isaiah 40:17.
[85] Jonah 3.

The firstborn son of Pharaoh was created in the image of God—just like every other man and woman on this earth. And he was just as much the object of God's love and blessings as any Hebrew captive. That is the nature of this God.

No, our God did not *want* to take the life of Pharaoh's firstborn son. *Taking* human life is never something the *Giver* of Life wants to do (or, for that matter, wants *anyone else* to do). When the Lord unleashed the Destroyer to enter the homes of the Egyptians that night, He did not do so with any sense of enjoyment or satisfaction. The destruction of Pharaoh's firstborn son was a painful sacrifice even for the God Who made it happen.

But God *did* make it happen. This God—*our* God—*did* take that life (and many others He did not desire to take) because He was determined to deliver the captives He had chosen as His own special people. He was determined to fulfill His promise of deliverance to them—and His plan of redemption *through* them and their experience of this inexplicable miracle. He was determined that Pharaoh would *let…His…people…go!* God was willing to sacrifice those firstborns to break *Pharaoh's* determination to block an Exodus that *God* was determined to accomplish.

This is a God willing to require great sacrifices—and make them Himself—when such sacrifices are necessary to realize His plan of salvation. He will deliver the captives He has determined to deliver, regardless the cost.

The Passover lamb and the firstborn son paid the price for the delivery of the captives from Egypt. But there would be another deliverance of captives to which God would commit Himself—and for that deliverance, *God* would supply both the Passover Lamb *and* the firstborn Son. *God* would pay for that deliverance.

☙❧

Fast forward 12 centuries—and "change." It is Passover time in the land to which God had delivered His chosen people. And just as Moses told the Hebrew leaders to prepare the Passover meal, so now a new and greater Moses tells those He has chosen to become leaders of a new Israel to do the same. Remember what we read in verses 7 and 8 of Luke 22: *"Then came the day of Unleavened Bread on which the Passover lamb had to be sacrificed. Jesus sent Peter and John, saying, 'Go and make preparations for us to eat the Passover.'"*

☙❧

This new Moses—this Jesus of Nazareth—will lead the new spiritual Israel out of their bondage to sin and death, and into a promised land of eternal joy and heavenly peace. But deliverance from sin and death is not without cost, either. And those held captive by the power of sin and death can no more pay the price of their liberation than could Hebrew slaves in Egypt have bought or fought their way out of Pharaoh's iron grip.

And so, a new generation of God's chosen people, captives in their own way, sit around a table of remembrance, recalling and reenacting the deliverance of old, and remembering the price that was paid to accomplish it.

Luke 22:14: *"When the hour came, Jesus and his apostles reclined at the table."*

There at that table sits a new and greater Moses, because *this* Moses, this Moses-named-Jesus, is also, at the same time, their Passover Lamb. He has come to be their worthy and sufficient Sacrifice, to provide the precious Blood that will shield and protect them from the destruction a righteous God will unleash on the sin that holds God's chosen ones captive.

Jesus is the new Moses. He is our Passover Lamb. And He is the firstborn and only begotten Son Whom the Father of Light has sent into the darkness of sin's captivity to break—through the sacrifice of His life—all worldly and other-worldly power committed to perpetuating the darkness and preventing the deliverance of those God *will…have…free!*

Delivery Charges

To deliver the Hebrews from bondage in Egypt, God *took* the life of Pharaoh's firstborn son. To deliver humanity from the bondage of sin, God *gives* the life of His *own* firstborn Son.

Does this firstborn Son understand His role—the responsibility His Heavenly Father has placed upon Him for our sakes? Here is Luke 22, verses 15 and 16: *"And he said to them, 'I have eagerly desired to eat this Passover with you before I suffer. For I tell you, I will not eat it again until it finds fulfillment in the kingdom of God.'"*

Yes, Jesus understands.

Fast-forward again: 2000 years and a *little* "change." You and I are invited to a table of remembrance and a time of recalling, of reenacting the experience of our deliverance from a captivity we could not escape. Today—here—you and I come and kneel before our Moses, our Passover Lamb, the firstborn Son Who paid the price for our deliverance from sin, and purchased our freedom from death itself by *His* death on the Cross.

As you come to the table of our Lord and partake of the bread and the cup He established, *"present your bodies as a living sacrifice..."*[86] to Him Who sacrificed all to pay the charges for your deliverance.

---

[86] Romans 12:1, RSV.

Jeremiah 31:31-34 ESV

³¹ "Behold, the days are coming, declares the LORD, when I will make a new covenant with the house of Israel and the house of Judah, ³² not like the covenant that I made with their fathers on the day when I took them by the hand to bring them out of the land of Egypt, my covenant that they broke, though I was their husband, declares the LORD. ³³ For this is the covenant that I will make with the house of Israel after those days, declares the LORD: I will put my law within them, and I will write it on their hearts. And I will be their God, and they shall be my people. ³⁴ And no longer shall each one teach his neighbor and each his brother, saying, 'Know the LORD,' for they shall all know me, from the least of them to the greatest, declares the LORD. For I will forgive their iniquity, and I will remember their sin no more."

Let's Try This Again

Luke 22:7-8, 13-20 ESV

⁷ Then came the day of Unleavened Bread, on which the Passover lamb had to be sacrificed. ⁸ So Jesus sent Peter and John, saying, "Go and prepare the Passover for us, that we may eat it."

¹³ And they went and found it just as he had told them, and they prepared the Passover.
¹⁴ And when the hour came, he reclined at table, and the apostles with him. ¹⁵ And he said to them, "I have earnestly desired to eat this Passover with you before I suffer. ¹⁶ For I tell you I will not eat it until it is fulfilled in the kingdom of God." ¹⁷ And he took a cup, and when he had given thanks he said, "Take this, and divide it among yourselves. ¹⁸ For I tell you that from now on I will not drink of the fruit of the vine until the kingdom of God comes." ¹⁹ And he took bread, and when he had given thanks, he broke it and gave it to them, saying, "This is my body, which is given for you. Do this in remembrance of me." ²⁰ And likewise the cup after they had eaten, saying, "This cup that is poured out for you is the new covenant in my blood."

6.

Let's Try This Again

Jeremiah 31:31-34; Luke 22:7-8, 13-20 ESV

Finding the prophecy (on the previous page) in the book of Jeremiah—a book in which page after page proclaims the doom of Judah and the destruction of Jerusalem—is like finding a twisted steel cross in the chaos of 9/11's Ground Zero,[87] or seeing a stone chapel standing, serene and undisturbed, beside the mountains of debris that had once been two great towers:[88] a moving message of hope buried in the rubble of a blown-apart world. Incredible. Inexplicable. Miraculous. And yet, there they were. And there the prophecy is.

Jeremiah's world was coming apart. The people of God had ignored the covenant God made with them at Mount Sinai. They had ignored the laws God gave them through Moses, obedience to which would have ensured God's blessings. They had banked on the promise of God to Abraham and David that He would bless their descendants no matter what they did.

---

[87] "The World Trade Center Cross," also known as "The Ground Zero Cross," was found in the debris of 6 World Trade Center and is believed to have been part of the North Tower.
[88] St. Paul's Chapel (Episcopal), now known as "The Little Chapel That Stood," is located across the street from where the South Tower had been.

But God's "no matter what" is not to be manipulated for sinful, selfish purposes. God is not mocked.[89] What they did *did* matter to God. And year after year, God poured out His judgment upon His disobedient people, as Jeremiah provided the pre-game predictions and the play-by-play analysis. But when the conclusion for God's sinful and rebellious people became clear, Jeremiah offered another (and unexpected) word from God: *"I will make a new covenant...."*

Their world came crashing down around them and there was nothing they could do to stop it. The time to do that had come and gone. They lost everything and were marched off into Exile with nothing but a word of hope: *"I will make a new covenant with [you]."* And they held on to that promise because they had nothing else to hold on to—every other promise had been frittered away.

They spent a lifetime in Exile, harboring the hope of a new covenant. They returned to their homeland, hoping this hope. Their children and grandchildren were born and lived and died, in good times (and more often, bad), looking for the fulfillment of the hope Jeremiah had given them so many years before. As kingdoms rose and fell—as their fortunes rose and fell—their hope was tested by hard times and hostile people and the delay in seeing the hope fulfilled.

Jeremiah had been right about God's *judgment*—right on the money. Would he not also be right about the *hope*? Were the days really coming—after so many days when nothing came to keep the promise and fulfill the hope? Would God ever make a new covenant with His people?

And then one day, there came a Carpenter. Not a king—or, at least, not a king you would recognize as such—but a Carpenter. A Carpenter came from the country where the people of God still

---

[89] Galatians 6:7.

Maundy Thursday

hoped the hope they had been given so many years—centuries—before. And the Carpenter told people—God's people—that the days that had been coming for so long—since Jeremiah—were here. The days had come in which God would make His new covenant—God would keep His promise—God would fulfill the hope.

But not everybody believed the Carpenter. Of course, not everybody had believed Jeremiah—about the judgment or the hope. Even some of those who had held onto the hope the tightest didn't believe the Carpenter. They didn't believe Him because the new covenant He announced was not just "new" in the sense of *replacing* the old; it was *different* from the old covenant.

And it turns out that even after all those years of hoping, a lot of people weren't prepared for the fulfillment of their hope to be provided in a different way than how they imagined it would be—even though God said the new covenant wouldn't be like the old one. They had spent all those years hoping for *their* dream-come-true, not God's.

❧

But the new covenant *was* different—*is* different. The old covenant was based on a set of laws—good laws, by the way—laws written on stones that people were "graded" on obeying—mainly, the important people—the big people—the people in charge.

The way this covenant worked was simple: obey the laws—get blessed; disobey the laws—get hammered. And even after everybody in Israel looked like a big bag of bent nails, they kept on disobeying God's laws.

So what was God to do? What He did was pull the plug on them—and then He promised them a new covenant as they went down the drain.

"So, Jeremiah, how does God say this new covenant will be new?"

Let's Try This Again

"God says,

> *'I will make this covenant...*
> *I will put My law within them...*
> *I will write it on their hearts...*
> *They will all know Me.'"*

Do you think God has figured out that we are not much good as covenant keepers—even the best of us?

If there's going to be a new covenant, God is going to have to make it, set it up, establish it. And He is going to have to make it work. We can't.

So what does God do to make a new covenant?

"I will put My law within them," He says. *"I will write it on their hearts."*

There's that "law" again—God's law. Before, it was rules—bunches of rules—dozens you could get killed for not obeying, and the "Ten Big Ones" God didn't even bother telling you what the punishment was for breaking. They wrote these laws on stones and then on scrolls. They put them up everywhere so people could learn them—in churches, schools and public places—though not so much now.

But the law of the new covenant will be written on human hearts.

Here's a thought: Do you suppose that God decided to write His law on our hearts because it was already written on His? And do you think that God's law is really, ultimately, all the rules they wrote down? Or are the rules really just a way to get at something more basic—more essentially divine—than that?

Do you think God's law could be something as simple as—well—unconditional, sacrificial love?

God told Jeremiah, *"I will put My law within them..."*

...which brings us back to the Carpenter.

Do you suppose that in order to "internalize" this new covenant for people—in order to write it on human hearts—God might wrap it up in one particular human Heart and put it within humanity that way?

Could God take His unconditional, sacrificial love and wrap it in a human Heart—like the heart of a Carpenter—and put that Carpenter into the world of people who couldn't keep a covenant with God if their lives depended on it, which, of course, they did—and do?

And could a Person—a Carpenter—with the law of God's great covenant love written in His heart—like it is in God's heart—somehow transfer that love of God as a law of love into the hearts of other people by loving them with that love so that they get that love written on their hearts, too?

And if that happened, would people who got loved by a Carpenter full of God's love love the Carpenter and everybody else so much that the love in them would keep the new covenant of God, even if they still couldn't keep all the very fine rules that made up the law code of the old covenant?

It might work that way because God told Jeremiah, *"I will forgive their wickedness and will remember their sins no more."* It really is a new covenant if God is going to take *that* approach.

So, is the Carpenter the key to this new covenant? He went from village to village and town to town with a love that either filled people with love themselves, if they let themselves be loved by Him—or repelled them, if they would not believe His was the Heart on which God had written His love for them.

And finally, the Carpenter went to the city were Jeremiah had delivered God's messages so long before. He gathered, not a multitude, but a modest group—not at the altar in the Temple, but around a table in an upper room—not to call down armies of angels, but to raise a cup, and offer it to them as the symbol of God's new covenant love: *"This cup is the new covenant in my blood, which is poured out for you."*

The cup of wine was the *symbol* of the new covenant, but the *substance* of the new covenant—the unconditional sacrifice of God's Heart of love—was the poured-out life of that Carpenter—that Christ—on a cross lifted high atop a mountain of sin and death.

For those who felt the love of this Carpenter Christ in their hearts, His Cross became the strong image of their new covenant with God, hope fulfilled amid the chaos of the world. And those who received the Carpenter's love became His Church, a holy structure that stood strong and undeterred by everything the evil prince of darkness tried to bring crashing down upon it.

Can a Carpenter be the Christ? Can a covenant with God be written in love on the hearts of sinful human beings? You will know the answer if you allow this Carpenter to be your Christ. You will know the truth of the prophet's hope if you open your heart to the covenant God would write upon it: the law of His love.

John 13:1-7, 31b-35 NRSV

¹ Now before the festival of the Passover, Jesus knew that his hour had come to depart from this world and go to the Father. Having loved his own who were in the world, he loved them to the end. ² The devil had already put it into the heart of Judas son of Simon Iscariot to betray him. And during supper ³ Jesus, knowing that the Father had given all things into his hands, and that he had come from God and was going to God, ⁴ got up from the table, took off his outer robe, and tied a towel around himself. ⁵ Then he poured water into a basin and began to wash the disciples' feet and to wipe them with the towel that was tied around him. ⁶ He came to Simon Peter, who said to him, "Lord, are you going to wash my feet?" ⁷ Jesus answered, "You do not know now what I am doing, but later you will understand."

³¹ …Jesus said, "Now the Son of Man has been glorified, and God has been glorified in him. ³² If God has been glorified in him, God will also glorify him in himself and will glorify him at once. ³³ Little children, I am with you only a little longer. You will look for me; and as I said to the Jews so now I say to you, 'Where I am going, you cannot come.' ³⁴ I give you a new commandment, that you love one another. Just as I have loved you, you also should love one another. ³⁵ By this everyone will know that you are my disciples, if you have love for one another."

7.

I Serve You; I Command You

John 13:1-7, 31b-35 NRSV

Now that there are digital cameras in smart phones and scanners hooked up to computers, you can do a lot more with pictures than you could in the old days, when all you could do was take a roll of film to be developed, and hope you got back something you could recognize. Now you can pull up a picture in your computer's memory and enlarge it or reduce it. You can flip it over. You can crop it so that you only see part of the whole picture.

I mention cropping pictures because we do the same thing with the Bible sometimes. We mentally "crop" the pictures the Bible provides us so that we look at one part—perhaps very intensely—and don't see another part at all.

How often have you come to Communion with the picture foremost in your mind of Jesus sitting at the center of a table, breaking bread and lifting up a cup of wine? *"This is my body.... This is my blood...."* Oh, what a powerful picture of His sacrifice for us!

But it is not the whole picture. The part of the picture of that last night and Last Supper with His disciples that our memories tend to crop out is the part in John 13 where Jesus gets up from the table, lays aside His outer garments, and begins to wash the feet of His stunned and very uncomfortable followers. "This is My water for washing. This is My towel for drying."

And it is every bit as powerful and accurate a picture of His sacrifice for us as the other one we always call to mind.

The bread represents His Body that will soon be broken for us. The wine in the cup represents His Blood that will soon be poured out to cover our sins. But Jesus has more to show His disciples in the symbols of His words and actions this night. There is more to the picture.

Jesus is willing to get up from the place of honor at the banquet table (a place that is His due as their undisputed Leader), just as He was willing to give up the place of honor that was His due in heaven as Son of God.[90] And just as He is willing to humble Himself and move from being the focus of their faces to the servant at their feet, so was He willing to forego the glory and praise of all the heavenly hosts to hobnob with beggars and lepers, prostitutes and crooks.[91]

Jesus takes off His outer garments and lays them down to serve the disciples—to cleanse them of the dirt of the day. In the same way, the following day, He will just as freely and willingly lay down His life, to cleanse them—and everyone else in the world—of the sin of a lifetime.

No Jew could be forced to wash a fellow Jew's feet. And these Jewish disciples are appalled to see Jesus bending over their feet with a basin and towel. But that's the picture Jesus wants them to see, so they will be able to see and understand the even more appalling picture of Jesus hanging on a criminal's cross.

Jesus humbles Himself to serve His disciples—to cleanse them. Jesus will humble Himself to die for His disciples—also to cleanse them—because (the Bible says), *"He loved them to the end"*— He loved them completely.

---

[90] Philippians 2:6-7.
[91] Matthew 9:10; Luke 7:37-39; 17:10-11; 19:5.

After He humbles Himself and serves them like a slave at dinner, He puts His garments back on and resumes His place—just as He will put His life back on after the Resurrection and take His rightful place at the right hand of God in heaven.[92] He serves His disciples and then He commands them: *"Love one another...as I have loved you."*

Do you see the picture? Not just "love one another" (in whatever way you personally conceive of love). Not even "love one another as *you* love *Me*" (even though they surely love Jesus very much). Jesus commands them—with an authority as compelling as the humility of His service to them: *"Love one another...as I have loved you."*

Why does Jesus give up His place and His dignity and His life to wash their feet and their lives clean?

Because He loves them in a completely unique and remarkable way—a way that He now commands them to replicate with one another.

Do you see the whole picture now? Complete submission in sacrificial service—full fellowship with Him in the sacred symbols of the believing community—challenging command to channel His love into every Christian relationship.

His Body.
His Blood.
His Basin.
His Towel.
His Life.
His Death.
His Sacrifice.
His Salvation.
His Love.
The whole picture.

---

[92] Romans 8:34.

8.

A Very Difficult Commandment

John 13:1-7, 31b-35 NRSV (p. 55)

There are a lot of things about the Christian life that sound hard. The Apostle Paul talks about moving mountains and voluntary martyrdom.[93] Jesus walked on water[94] and raised people from the dead.[95] That sounds hard.

By comparison, *"love one another,"* sounds easy. It sounds lofty and inspiring.

You may be thinking: "Let's skip the 'water walking' and 'mountain moving' and focus on love. *'Love one another.'* That sounds good."

Good?

Yes.

Easy?

Not on your life!

ৰ–্ব

---

[93] 1 Corinthians 13:1-3.
[94] Matthew 14:25.
[95] John 11:43-44.

"Love one another" is not an idea Jesus offered to inspire you. It is a command—an order—and it has proven to be a very difficult one to obey.

Look what's going on: Jesus has gathered His disciples in a secret room. There are those who want to kill Him, and He and His followers must hide so that death will not come too soon.

In this borrowed haven, Jesus has shared a meal with them—the meal we share today. But the mood there is not lofty and inspiring, as ours is here. The atmosphere in that room reeks of confusion and fear. The Leader has broken bread and passed a cup of wine, speaking solemn words of sacrifice and death. The One they call "Master" has knelt down before each of them like a slave and washed their feet.

And if they are stunned by His unexpected act of humility, they are undone by His revelation that there is a traitor among them—in that very room. As they grapple with this "bombshell," Jesus reaches out to His betrayer—whose feet He has just washed—with still another intimate expression of love.

But the betrayer will not accept His love. And so, rejecting the Light of the world, a disciple whom Jesus loves goes out into the darkness—out into the night.

୧ଓ

He will go to the enemy and lead them to the Lord. And then the greatest battle of all time will begin. The ultimate war between good and evil will be waged in the palace of a priest and across the patio of Pilate, on the spikes of a cross and within a borrowed tomb.

But before the battle begins, God's greatest Warrior gathers His troops and gives them their final orders: *"Love one another."* Jesus is about to step off into the night, invading the enemy's territory and joining the fight He was sent by God to win. And win it He will.

But it is a suicide mission; it will take His life to accomplish it. And so before He goes, He must give His little squad—His dozen minus one—their marching orders. For they have a mission to perform in this struggle as well.

And the orders do not change, even when the squad becomes a company and the company, a battalion—when the battalion becomes a division and the division, an army beyond number, stationed around the globe. To each new recruit—to every disciple—to all His troops—Jesus gives the same order: *"Love one another."*

"I give you a new commandment, that you love one another."

Simple?

Yes, the best orders are. But "simple" does not mean "easy to carry out." This is an amazingly difficult commandment to obey.

And why is that?

One reason is that Jesus makes it specific. He is not saying, "Love everybody." It is true that *"God so loved the world that He gave His only-begotten Son."*[96] But that's not what Jesus is commanding them—and us—to do here.

It seems relatively easy to love the whole world-in-general. Of course, only God can do that in any meaningful way, so our efforts on that scale will be rather impersonal and, therefore, fairly safe. Love the whole world?

Certainly. Consider it done.

But that's not the new commandment.

Jesus says to His disciples, *"Love **one another.**"* The command is to Christians. The command is about Christians. The command is for Christians to love Christians—and, particularly, the ones with whom you are most closely and frequently associated.

---

[96] John 3:16, KJV.

It is wonderful to know that Jesus loves you. It is natural that, knowing this, you would love Jesus right back.

But loving one another is a different thing entirely—or so it seems. Christians—even the ones in this church—are not as wonderful as Jesus. The people sitting around you are not as holy and perfect as the Lord we all love. The folks on our committees and in our Bible studies are not always as wise and winsome as the Son of God Who is the Source of our salvation. Even without Judas, the disciples weren't always a loving band of brothers.[97]

Why is it so hard for us as Christians to love one another?

Besides the fact that it is remarkably easy to hurt our feelings or get our dander up—besides the fact that we tend to apply tougher standards to others than we do to ourselves—besides the fact that we get focused on our own agendas and lose sight of God's big picture—besides the fact that the devil doesn't want us to love one another and does everything he can to keep us from doing so—besides all that, loving one another is work. It just doesn't come naturally when we are sinful, and the people we are commanded to love are sinful, too.

☙❧

But that's what Jesus says to do—and He says more: *"Love one another... **as I have loved you.**"* Jesus has just gotten down on His knees to love His disciples. He is hours away from laying down His life to love them.

Paul told Christian husbands to love their wives *"as Christ loved the Church—**and gave Himself up for her.**"*[98] According to Paul, the love with which we are to love one another as Christians is patient and kind, trusting and humble and gracious. It is selfless and serene and accepting—bearing, believing, hoping and

---

[97] Mark 10:35-41.
[98] Ephesians 5:25, ESV.

enduring endlessly.[99] That kind of love makes our Lord's command a very difficult one to fulfill.

And yet, He commands us: *"Love one another."*

Why does He give us such a difficult commandment? Why couldn't He just say, "Love Me—and be as good as you can"?

That would be a whole lot easier. A lot of us have already settled for that anyway as our self-assigned mission as Christians.

But *"Love one another"* is His command, and *"as I have loved you"* is the way He wants the command carried out. And the reason He has commanded us to love one another is that, *"by this, everyone will know that* [we] *are* [His] *disciples."*

☙❧

When Jesus gave this order to His disciples, He was going into battle. He gave this order because He was leading His disciples into battle as well. And what you need to know is that *"love one another"* is not a "hold the fort" kind of order; it is a "take the hill" kind of order.

Jesus led His disciples out of that safe house and into the dark and dangerous world because He was sent to win God's war against sin, and in doing so, to win the world back to God. Jesus defeated sin and death, and His disciples are His instruments for winning back the world—not by our superior saintliness, but by our sacrificial love.

We march through this life—through this world—as God's liberating army, not because we are good, but because we love one another in a way that cannot be done in this world apart from His love, for us and in us.

And when they see *that*—when those who are not Christians see us loving one another with a love that we do not deserve and could not come up with on our own—those who remain in the darkness of this world will see a Light that is not of this world—

---

[99] 1 Corinthians 13:4-8.

the Light of God's liberating love. As long as we love one another as He has loved us, the world is confronted with the love of Jesus.

Still, it is an amazingly difficult commandment, given who we are. It would be impossible for us to obey, except for Who Jesus is, and the fact that He provides the love in the first place.

"Love one another," He said.

It won't be easy. It's never easy. But we *have* to do it. And we *can* do it. We *can* love one another, with God's help.

9.

Treachery at the Table

John 13:21-30 RSV

²¹ When Jesus had thus spoken, he was troubled in spirit, and testified, "Truly, truly, I say to you, one of you will betray me." ²² The disciples looked at one another, uncertain of whom he spoke. ²³ One of his disciples, whom Jesus loved, was lying close to the breast of Jesus; ²⁴ so Simon Peter beckoned to him and said, "Tell us who it is of whom he speaks." ²⁵ So lying thus, close to the breast of Jesus, he said to him, "Lord, who is it?" ²⁶ Jesus answered, "It is he to whom I shall give this morsel when I have dipped it." So when he had dipped the morsel, he gave it to Judas, the son of Simon Iscariot. ²⁷ Then after the morsel, Satan entered into him. Jesus said to him, "What you are going to do, do quickly." ²⁸ Now no one at the table knew why he said this to him. ²⁹ Some thought that, because Judas had the money box, Jesus was telling him, "Buy what we need for the feast"; or, that he should give something to the poor. ³⁰ So, after receiving the morsel, he immediately went out; and it was night.

☙❧

Communion is a beautiful event: Christians gathered in joy and serenity around the table of our Lord; morsels of bread and a cup of wine (or grape juice, perhaps); the familiar, sacred words repeated in reverence: *"Take. Eat. This is my body...."*[100]

The Lord's Supper is a holy and inspiring event for the disciples of Christ.

❧

But it didn't start out that way.

The last meal Jesus shared with His disciples was neither joyful nor serene. The bread and the wine were there, but the mood was anything but inspiring. The tension hung heavy, and everybody would have been reaching for the Rolaids, if there had been any.

And Jesus wasn't helping the situation. Everything He did and said was a shocker. He got down on His knees like a common slave and washed their feet. Then He announced, matter-of-factly, *"One of you will betray me."*[101] The dinner was not getting off to a great start.

They knew there were enemies outside. They had seen them up close, and barely escaped them more than once. But inside, with Jesus, they're supposed to be safe. They're His followers—His disciples. And yet, in their midst—around that table—behind one of those familiar faces—there is a traitor.

Nobody's thinking about it being a "sacred hour."[102] They're wondering who it could be, and how it could be, and what are they going to do.

"Lord, who is it?"

Do you ask Him?

Does He know?

❧

Jesus knows.

---

[100] Matthew 26:26, RSV.
[101] Matthew 26:21, RSV.
[102] See "Here at Thy Table, Lord," verse 1, May P. Hoyt, 1889.

Maundy Thursday

Everyone is deceived, except Jesus. An insider—a disciple—is going to betray Him. His friends have no idea. The traitor is putting on an act of love and loyalty, but Jesus knows what's in his heart. Jesus knows what's in every human heart.

Jesus knows that Judas is the traitor—but Jesus doesn't treat Judas like the traitor Jesus knows him to be. Jesus has abased Himself to wash the feet of Judas. He has placed Judas at the place of honor beside Him at the table. Jesus has offered Judas the sign of special respect and affection by handing him food.

Jesus does not stop loving Judas, even though He knows what Judas has in his heart to do. Even as Judas is breaking away, Jesus is reaching out to him in love and with grace, inviting Judas to come back into the light of His presence. But Jesus lets Judas do what Judas is determined to do.

Jesus could stop Judas from going out into the darkness, but He does not. Jesus could prevent Judas from betraying Him into the hands of His enemies, but Jesus does not do that, either. Jesus could have kept Judas from causing His torture and crucifixion, but Jesus allows Judas to do what Judas has made up his mind to do.

Judas will not be drawn back to the light and love of Jesus—even by Jesus. Judas accepts the morsel Jesus gives him—but not the love with which it is given. Judas is rejecting God's gift of light and life. Even before he leaves the room, the darkness envelops Judas.

It is always night for one who is created by God when he rejects God and goes out into the world without God. And in the dark without a light, a man always gets lost. Judas will go out into the night—into the darkness—to betray Jesus.

And he will destroy himself in the process.

꙳

"Well, at least we're not as bad as Judas!" you may think.

Oh, really? And if that were true, of what significance would the distinction be. It's like saying we tried to get a little higher on the TITANIC as it was sinking in the night.

Judas betrayed Jesus. Peter denied Him. All the others deserted Him. All the disciples of Jesus have fallen away at one time or another—even us.

❧

But—praise God!—Jesus loves all His disciples better than any disciple deserves.

It was because of the "Judas nature" in all of us that Jesus gave up His place of heavenly honor in the bosom of His divine Father[103] to draw the likes of Judas—and us—to a similar place of honor next to Him. What the eternal Son of God deserved, by His divine and holy nature, He offered to us undeserving sinners—a gift of pure and radiant grace.

Jesus used a tender act of affection to identify His betrayer. And it is with that same tender affection that Jesus—betrayed, and crucified for our sins—forgives our failures of devotion and obedience, and invites us to be cleansed by His Blood, and fed by Him Who is the Bread of Life.

Jesus humbled Himself like a servant to wash away your uncleanness. He gives you a place beside Him. He offers you spiritual Food—living Bread. He invites you to come out of the darkness and into His light.

❧

As Jews, they were commemorating the Passover, a night when the people of God stayed inside, protected by the blood of a lamb from the death that hovered in the darkness outside.

---

[103] Philippians 2:6-7.

But the Light shines in the darkness. In that tiny room, the Light of the world still shines and prepares the faithful for the contest with darkness, and the victory over it, that is to come.

Jesus tells Judas, *"What you are going to do, do quickly."* Most assume He means for Judas to get on with the business of betrayal. But perhaps Jesus is urging Judas, even now, to quickly decide to choose the light instead of darkness.

"Until you go out into the darkness, there is still light. Let us embrace the Light that overcomes the darkness, without and within.

2 Samuel 15:13-30 ESV

13 And a messenger came to David, saying, "The hearts of the men of Israel have gone after Absalom." 14 Then David said to all his servants who were with him at Jerusalem, "Arise, and let us flee, or else there will be no escape for us from Absalom. Go quickly, lest he overtake us quickly and bring down ruin on us and strike the city with the edge of the sword." 15 And the king's servants said to the king, "Behold, your servants are ready to do whatever my lord the king decides." 16 So the king went out, and all his household after him. And the king left ten concubines to keep the house. 17 And the king went out, and all the people after him. And they halted at the last house.

18 And all his servants passed by him, and all the Cherethites, and all the Pelethites, and all the six hundred Gittites who had followed him from Gath, passed on before the king. 19 Then the king said to Ittai the Gittite, "Why do you also go with us? Go back and stay with the king, for you are a foreigner and also an exile from your home. 20 You came only yesterday, and shall I today make you wander about with us, since I go I know not where? Go back and take your brothers with you, and may the LORD show steadfast love and faithfulness to you." 21 But Ittai answered the king, "As the LORD lives, and as my lord the king lives, wherever my lord the king shall be, whether for death or for life, there also will your servant be." 22 And David said to Ittai, "Go then, pass on." So Ittai the Gittite passed on with all his men and all the little ones who were with him. 23 And all the land wept aloud as all the people passed by, and the king crossed the brook Kidron, and all the people passed on toward the wilderness.

24 And Abiathar came up, and behold, Zadok came also with all the Levites, bearing the ark of the covenant of God. And they set down the ark of God until the people had all passed out of the city. 25 Then the king said to Zadok, "Carry the ark of God back into the city. If I find favor in the eyes of the LORD, he will bring me back and let me see both it and his dwelling place. 26 But if he says, 'I have no pleasure in you,' behold, here I am, let him do to me what seems good to him." 27 The king also said to Zadok the priest, "Are you not a seer? Go back to the city in peace, with your two sons, Ahimaaz

Maundy Thursday

your son, and Jonathan the son of Abiathar. ²⁸ See, I will wait at the fords of the wilderness until word comes from you to inform me." ²⁹ So Zadok and Abiathar carried the ark of God back to Jerusalem, and they remained there.

³⁰ But David went up the ascent of the Mount of Olives, weeping as he went, barefoot and with his head covered. And all the people who were with him covered their heads, and they went up, weeping as they went.

Mark 14:32-36 ESV

[32] And they went to a place called Gethsemane. And [Jesus] said to his disciples, "Sit here while I pray." [33] And he took with him Peter and James and John, and began to be greatly distressed and troubled. [34] And he said to them, "My soul is very sorrowful, even to death. Remain here and watch." [35] And going a little farther, he fell on the ground and prayed that, if it were possible, the hour might pass from him. [36] And he said, "Abba, Father, all things are possible for you. Remove this cup from me. Yet not what I will, but what you will."

10.

Hope in the Darkness

2 Samuel 15:13-30; Mark 14:32-36 ESV

The geography of old Jerusalem hasn't changed much in two thousand years—or, for that matter, in three. Just as tourists today flock to the Holy Land to walk in the footsteps of Jesus, so Jesus would have been very conscious of the fact that He was walking where His ancestor David had walked, especially when He was in and around Jerusalem.

The architecture was different, of course: there was no Temple there in David's day. And much of what David and Solomon had built was gone by the time Jesus got there, replaced by the more recent works of Herod and the Romans. But "the lay of the land" was much the same, with the Kidron Valley dropping off to the east of the Temple Mount. And beyond that, the Garden of Gethsemane nestled at the base of the Mount of Olives.

And both Jesus and David before Him made their way through that valley in their darkest hours, with nothing short of death itself breathing down their necks. And each in his own way would offer the same prayer in that sacred place: "Deliver me from the danger that's closing in on me, if You will, Lord. But regardless, Your will be done."

We'll come back to Jesus in a moment (as everyone should).

But, for now, let's join David as disaster destroys the illusion of his pleasant and well-protected world. Everything is "fine," as far as he knows. And then a messenger arrives with very bad news. With one sentence, David's wonderful world is no more.

※

It can happen that fast.

You've been there. Someone you love says, "I'm leaving." The doctor gives you "the last news in the world you want to hear." Your child goes off the deep end despite all your efforts.

Disaster! And it's yours, and you've got to live with it!

So what do you do?

You can't turn back the clock or rewind the film. The genie is out of the bottle.

What *can* you do?

David does a number of things when he learns that his son, Absalom, has betrayed him and that the people David had delivered from their oppressors have now joined his son in rebellion. These are horrible things to experience. It's the kind of thing that makes you want to roll over and die.

Absalom has *"the men of Israel"* behind him. David has only the palace guard and the household staff and a few well-wishers who happen to be in town or hanging out nearby. This time, Chicken Little is right: "The sky *is* falling." And it must have felt to King David, "like the moon, the stars and all the planets just fell on [him]"—to borrow Harry Truman's words.[104]

But when David hears the news, he assesses the problem—and does what he can do. Hard and heartbreaking as his new reality is, he acts immediately to minimize the impact of what has happened.

He is terribly vulnerable, but he is not alone. In a crisis, some people will step up to help—and some will step out of the line of

---

[104] Harry Truman's first comment to reporters about his reaction to learning of the death of Franklin D. Roosevelt and his own elevation to the office of President, Washington, DC, April 13, 1945.

fire. Bless those who bless you, and let them do for you what they can. Ignore those who drop away. And don't worry about who falls in which category.

David organizes himself and those who stick with him for survival, even though he cannot *guarantee* that survival—much less success—will be the result of what they do. He isn't giving up or giving in to despair as he leads those loyal to him out of the city. Like the Marine Corps general at Korea's Chosin Reservoir, surrounded by an overwhelming enemy force, King David is "attacking in a different direction."[105] David is adapting to a new—if undesirable—reality and putting himself in the best position to deal with the mess that has dropped in his lap.

And notice that when he talks about the danger and what must be done about it, all the pronouns are plural:
> *"Let **us** flee…or there will be no escape for **us**.…*
> *Hurry, or he'll catch **us** and do bad things to **us**."*

Though Absalom is after David and his throne—making the crisis seem very personal—David understands that many people are there to help him, and his darkness is their darkness, too.

David and his people march away from the old "normal" so they can respond better to the "new terrible." With Absalom and his forces on the way, David and his friends walk through the valley of the shadow of death—as we do, when difficulty strikes, and darkness descends upon us.

⁂

And here's another thing: Though they do what they have to do without delay, they do not pretend that they like it.

When disaster strikes, you grieve, even while you're doing what you can about it—if there's anything you can do.

---

[105] Brigadier General Oliver Stone, Commander of the 1st Marine Division, November 1950, though the comment is often attributed to Colonel "Chesty" Puller, who was Commander of the 1st Regiment of the 1st Division at the time.

Everybody is crying. David is crying. They are grown men—strong men—crying out loud—in public! They don't care; their world is coming apart. David and everybody else go out of the city with their feet bare and their heads covered—like mourners going to a funeral. You don't have to act like a catastrophe is "okay" when it's anything but. A good cry about a bad thing can be a good thing.

॰৯

But here's what I really want you to see: the priests and the Levites bring the Ark of the Covenant out of Jerusalem so this sacred symbol of God can lead the beleaguered king's impromptu parade. As far as they are concerned, David brought the Ark into the city "way back when;" and he has the right to carry it out now. If David has the Ark with him—they reason—then, surely, he must have God on his side—or, at least, that's what they want the people who see it and hear about it to think.

But David does an interesting thing: he orders them to take the Ark back into the city where they got it.

And David *says* an interesting thing, by way of explanation: "If I find favor in the Lord's eyes, He will bring me back and let me see it again."

David's kingdom is coming apart—which would suggest to the casual observer that David has lost any chance of "favor in God's eyes."

The medieval Italian poet Dante wrote a book about the afterlife as he imagined it,[106] and above the entrance to hell was a sign that read, "Abandon all hope, ye who enter here."

You would think a similar sign could have been posted for David as he passed through the gates of his capital city: "Abandon all hope, kings who flee from here."

---

[106] Dante Alighieri, *The Divine Comedy*, Part I: "Inferno," 1320.

But David will not take this advice. In his darkest hour—in his most desperate crisis—David lets go of the "symbol" of God in his possession and reaches out for the reality of God that neither he nor anyone else can ever possess in that way.

*"**If** I find favor with God...* I don't know if I will, but I will take my chances with God. I will do everything I can, but I know that, ultimately, it all depends on God, so *I* am depending on God—trusting God in the depths of the darkness."

And *that*, my friends, is what the Bible means by "hope."

☙❧

Why would David put his hope in God? Yes, David had found favor with God a lot in his life. But over time, David had also done a lot of things that had to have gone in God's "*un*-favorable column." Is this just David "playing the odds?"

No, this is David, who knows enough about God to believe that hope in this God is a winning strategy in a crisis you can't control yourself: "When I can't make my way work—and things aren't going the way I want them to—I'm willing to go with God."

It's like the song says,

> "Through many dangers, toils and snares,
> I have already come.
> Tis grace hath brought me safe thus far,
> and grace will lead me home."[107]

King David didn't write that song, but he could have.

Hope is what allows us to say with the Apostle Paul: *"We are afflicted in every way, but not crushed; perplexed, but not despairing; persecuted, but not forsaken; struck down, but not destroyed...."*[108]

Paul also said, *"...we rejoice in hope of the glory of God. Not only that, but we rejoice in our sufferings, knowing that suffering produces endurance, and endurance produces character, and character produces hope, and hope does not*

---

[107] John Newton, "Amazing Grace," *Olney Hymns*, Olney, England, 1779.
[108] 2 Corinthians 4:8-9, ESV.

put us to shame, because God's love has been poured into our hearts through the Holy Spirit who has been given to us."[109]

We go into our darkness with hope, and we learn to love the hope and how it helps us in our dark times. And we even come to appreciate that—because of our hope—we can find God and His favor *in* our darkness, sorrow and suffering—in a way that we *never* could in "the good times" we prefer.

Did David find the favor with God he hoped for?

Yes, he did. He returned to Jerusalem and his throne—and to the Ark of the Covenant.

Did he deserve to find God's favor?

Honestly, no. But that is what hope knows: You can find favor with God without deserving it, because of Who our God is. David should have died, but he didn't. God brought him out of the darkness and back to life...

❧

...which brings us back to David's divine Descendent, Jesus.

Jesus retraced those royal footsteps on the night that He was betrayed. Jesus went out of the city as far as the Garden of Gethsemane, and there the God in Whom He put *His* hope ordered "Halt!" There in the darkness, a beloved disciple would kiss Jesus into the hands of His enemies, and, ultimately, onto a cross.

Unlike David, Jesus will return to the city the same night He leaves it, and overcome a far worse rebellion than David faced by giving Himself as a sacrifice to those who have sought to kill Him, dying in a darkness that covers not just Him, but the whole world,[110] and finding God's favor in forgiving those who could never find God's favor apart from Him.[111]

---

[109] Romans 5:2b-5, ESV.
[110] Matthew 27:45.
[111] Luke 23:34.

David lets go of His hold on Jerusalem, and in the darkness of his despair, puts his hope in God.

Jesus lets go of His hold on life, hoping—believing—that, in the darkness of death, He will find favor with God.

And now we who endure the darkness of the hurts and hardships of this life—and death that comes in the end—have the opportunity to put our hope in God, and, in doing so, to find His favor, as a restored David and our Risen Lord did.

"Hope does not disappoint," says Paul[112]—if you put your hope in the grace of God.

---

[112] Romans 5:5, RSV.

Good Friday

John 18:28—19:16 RSV

18 *²⁸ Then they led Jesus from the house of Ca'iaphas to the praetorium. It was early. They themselves did not enter the praetorium, so that they might not be defiled, but might eat the passover. ²⁹ So Pilate went out to them and said, "What accusation do you bring against this man?" ³⁰ They answered him, "If this man were not an evildoer, we would not have handed him over." ³¹ Pilate said to them, "Take him yourselves and judge him by your own law." The Jews said to him, "It is not lawful for us to put any man to death." ³² This was to fulfil the word which Jesus had spoken to show by what death he was to die.*

³³ Pilate entered the praetorium again and called Jesus, and said to him, "Are you the King of the Jews?" ³⁴ Jesus answered, "Do you say this of your own accord, or did others say it to you about me?" ³⁵ Pilate answered, "Am I a Jew? Your own nation and the chief priests have handed you over to me; what have you done?" ³⁶ Jesus answered, "My kingship is not of this world; if my kingship were of this world, my servants would fight, that I might not be handed over to the Jews; but my kingship is not from the world." ³⁷ Pilate said to him, "So you are a king?" Jesus answered, "You say that I am a king. For this I was born, and for this I have come into the world, to bear witness to the truth. Every one who is of the truth hears my voice." ³⁸ Pilate said to him, "What is truth?"

After he had said this, he went out to the Jews again, and told them, "I find no crime in him. ³⁹ But you have a custom that I should release one man for you at the Passover; will you have me release for you the King of the Jews?" ⁴⁰ They cried out again, "Not this man, but Barab'bas!" Now Barab'bas was a robber.

19 *¹ Then Pilate took Jesus and scourged him. ² And the soldiers plaited a crown of thorns, and put it on his head, and arrayed him in a purple robe; ³ they came up to him, saying, "Hail, King of the Jews!" and struck him with their hands. ⁴ Pilate went out again, and said to them, "See, I am bringing him out to you, that you may know that I find no crime in him." ⁵ So Jesus came out, wearing the crown of thorns and the purple robe. Pilate said to them,*

"Behold the man!" ⁶ *When the chief priests and the officers saw him, they cried out, "Crucify him, crucify him!" Pilate said to them, "Take him yourselves and crucify him, for I find no crime in him."* ⁷ *The Jews answered him, "We have a law, and by that law he ought to die, because he has made himself the Son of God."* ⁸ *When Pilate heard these words, he was the more afraid;* ⁹ *he entered the praetorium again and said to Jesus, "Where are you from?" But Jesus gave no answer.* ¹⁰ *Pilate therefore said to him, "You will not speak to me? Do you not know that I have power to release you, and power to crucify you?"* ¹¹ *Jesus answered him, "You would have no power over me unless it had been given you from above; therefore he who delivered me to you has the greater sin."*

¹² *Upon this Pilate sought to release him, but the Jews cried out, "If you release this man, you are not Caesar's friend; every one who makes himself a king sets himself against Caesar."* ¹³ *When Pilate heard these words, he brought Jesus out and sat down on the judgment seat at a place called The Pavement, and in Hebrew, Gab'batha.* ¹⁴ *Now it was the day of Preparation of the Passover; it was about the sixth hour. He said to the Jews, "Behold your King!"* ¹⁵ *They cried out, "Away with him, away with him, crucify him!" Pilate said to them, "Shall I crucify your King?" The chief priests answered, "We have no king but Caesar."* ¹⁶ *Then he handed him over to them to be crucified.*

11.

Trying Questions

John 18:28—19:16 RSV

As Christians, we confess that Jesus Christ died for our sins. But Jesus did not merely die; He was executed. We proclaim that Jesus gave His life freely as a ransom for many, but it is also true that He was tortured and killed on the order of the duly appointed government official in charge, after a public trial conducted according to the established legal procedures for that time and place.

The trial was conducted, and the execution order given, by a minor Roman politician named Pontius Pilate. Mr. Pilate ran the Roman occupation of Judea for about ten years with little success and less thanks, and then disappeared into the haze of antiquity.

But on this one spring day in Jerusalem, Pilate will stand at the greatest crossroads in the history of mankind. Pilate will question and then pass judgment (he thinks) on one more of those religious fanatics the region is so famous for, a charismatic Carpenter from some squalid little village in Galilee, Whose death (as it turns out) will change the world forever.

The Gospel of John tells us more about the encounter between Jesus and Pilate, Defendant and judge, than do the other gospels. And as is often the case with John, more is being said here than what the words actually say. We will have to consider not just the simple facts presented, but the deeper truth implied. And if you will permit me, I will highlight the most significant verses for our purposes today, rather than plowing us through the entire lengthy passage.

The arrest and trial of Jesus take up most of Chapters 18 and 19 of John. After Jesus is taken into custody by a combination of Roman soldiers and Jewish Temple police, He is questioned throughout the night by the Jewish religious leaders. Early the next morning, Jesus is taken, bound, to Pilate.

Let's pick up the scene in Chapter 18, verse 33, where Pilate first encounters Jesus, and read through verse 38.

❧

Pilate's first (and final) impression is that Jesus is an innocent Man. But the "prosecution" outside will have none of this and they ratchet up the pressure on Pilate to "do Jesus in." In response, Pilate orders Jesus tortured, and his torturers throw in some vicious ridicule for free. Pilate actually intends this as a favor for Jesus, hoping to drum up sympathy for Him. Jesus is brought out half dead, but half dead is not enough for those who are determined that Jesus must be completely dead—crucified and buried.

Frustrated at the way the mob has controlled him, and fearful of the political damage they can still do him, Pilate returns to Jesus. Look at Chapter 19, verses 9 through 11.

❧

Getting nowhere with Jesus, Pilate goes back out to the well-organized mob, who once again out-wit and out-maneuver him at every turn. With every pretense of authority and justice surrendered, Pilate finally discards his honor as well, and consoles his pride in a parting blast of sarcasm. *"Then,"* according to verse 16, *"...he handed him over to them to be crucified."*

There is much we could say about this encounter between Jesus and Pilate—too much to be said in one sermon.

For now, look with me at the questions Pilate puts to Jesus. John records seven:

"Are you the King of the Jews?"
"Am I a Jew?"
"What have you done?"
"What is truth?"
"Where are you from?"
"You will not speak to me?"
"Do you not know that I have power to release you, and power to crucify you?"

❧

Some of these questions Jesus answers. Some He ignores. In no case does Jesus give Pilate a response that indicates guilt. Nothing justifies the sentence Pilate imposes. The questions tell us as much about Pilate as the answers tell us about Jesus.

As he conducts the trial, Pilate is not just judging Jesus, he is being judged himself, by those inside the palace with him and by the religious leaders waiting outside, by the Roman hierarchy that will, in time, review the reports of this trial—and by the God and Father of Jesus Christ, Who sent His Son to reveal His truth.

Some of the questions Pilate puts to Jesus are reasonable and appropriate lines of inquiry, necessary to prove or disprove the changes brought against Him: "Jesus, are You a violent revolutionary? Are You a risk to the stability of the order Rome has imposed here? Have Your actions or Your associations marked You as a threat to peace and prosperity?"

Other questions demonstrate Pilate's personal surprise and exasperation with this Prisoner Who dares to question *him* and shows no concern about what verdict Pilate will pronounce: "Am I a Jew? Why won't You answer me? Don't You know I can kill You or set You free?"

And right in the middle of all these questions, Pilate confronts, if only for a moment, the possibility that there is a reality "beyond"—beyond his vision, his understanding, his control: "What is truth?"

॰◦॰

Someone has said, "When court is in session, everybody is on trial." Jesus stands before Pilate, who will render a verdict on Him. At the same time, Pilate stands before Jesus, and it is Pilate who is being weighed in the balance. But there is more: *every*body is on trial.

This is our day in court, too. Today, we may judge. One day, we will be the defendants. One day, we will stand before the heavenly throne and the King will render His judgment on us. But today, the evidence is presented *to* you and me. *We* hear the testimony. *We* consider the questions of the case.

Jesus isn't brought to us in a Roman praetorium, of course. Our verdict is demanded on the school grounds and at work, where we shop and where we play. With the hostile world outside and Jesus inside, we confront the same questions Pilate raised, in spirit if not in actual wording. Listen again to these "trying" questions—questions that determine our verdict about Jesus—and His about us.

॰◦॰

"Is Jesus the King of the Jews?" Pilate wanted to know. "Is Jesus a threat to my power?"

For us, the question can be rephrased slightly, "Is Jesus sovereign?" Is He a king? Is He the descendent of King David sent by God in fulfillment of promise and prophecy to rule over God's people?

The world recognizes that Jesus makes such a claim, and condemns it as absolute and intolerant, ridiculing anyone who supports it. How do you answer the question?

Jesus personalizes the issue of His sovereignty with Pilate, and Pilate reacts in amazement: "Am I a Jew?" The answer that seems so obvious when Pilate first blurts out the question seems far less so after he has been driven so effectively by the Jewish religious leaders to renounce all his Roman ideals and responsibilities and *kow-tow* to the agenda they propose.

How do we ask the question appropriately today? Perhaps, "Am I subject to the authority of Jesus?" If your answer to the first question is "yes," then the answer to the second will depend on what you understand "the people of God" to mean. Jesus may be a King, but is He *your* King?

When Pilate wanted to get the focus of the trial of Jesus back on Jesus, he asked Him, "What have You done?" The part of the question Pilate left unspoken was, "...that would justify my finding You guilty and punishing You?"

༒

For you and me, the question extends a different way: "What has Jesus done that would demonstrate His sovereignty and justify our submission to it?" What has Jesus done for God? What has Jesus done for us?

Pilate continues to be amazed at this Man Who is more interested in an elusive, nebulous concept like "truth" than the real and practical power inherent in being a king. How Pilate asked the question, we do not know. But the very fact that he asked the question of Jesus is the significant reality. Unfortunately, he did not wait around for the answer.

Pilate is stunned that Jesus is not concerned to defend Himself from the untruth told about Him, while He *is* concerned to confront Pilate with the claims of truth. By this time, the trial is no longer about the innocence or guilt of Jesus; it is about whether Pilate will respond to the truth before him.

We do well to put this question to Jesus ourselves in a day when everything is true—or nothing is. We ask anybody and everybody about truth today. In our world, the truth changes day by day. But if we were to put the question to Jesus, and wait upon His answer, what would we hear? "Jesus, what is truth?"

☙❧

The last three questions Pilate put to Jesus, he asked when the answers no longer mattered. The trial was over. The judge had been weighed in the balance, with his courage and his integrity found wanting. The fate of Jesus had been sealed, not by the findings of the judge in court, but by the clamoring of His enemies beyond the wall.

Pilate never wanted to be bothered with this Jesus business. Yes, he helped the "Temple mafia" arrest Jesus. But Pilate just wanted to avoid trouble, and Jesus had all the markings of a "trouble magnet."

"Just lock Him down somewhere out of sight till all the tourists go home and the excitement is over. Rough Him up a little bit, if you need to, to keep Him quiet and teach Him who's boss. But let's not get all worked up over some Galilean Peasant with a charismatic personality and a unique take on His religious heritage."

Pilate tries to adopt a middle position about Jesus—neither hostility nor faith. But neutrality regarding Jesus never works. Not then—not now.

These last three questions are not to be ignored in our consideration of Jesus. Certainly, God will evaluate the answers we give them. The questions boil down to these: "Where did Jesus come from?" "What does Jesus have to say to us?" and "What will we do with Jesus?"

Remember that when you are evaluating Jesus, judging whether Jesus should live in your life—in your world—or not, you are passing judgment on yourself at the same time. Remember that you are providing evidence in your life that others will consider when they come to answer the trying questions about Jesus.

Good Friday

Court is in session.
What is *your* verdict regarding Jesus…
…and *His*, regarding *you*?

Our Evil—God's Good

Genesis 45:1-8; 50:15-20 ESV

45 *¹ Then Joseph could not control himself before all those who stood by him. He cried, "Make everyone go out from me." So no one stayed with him when Joseph made himself known to his brothers. ² And he wept aloud, so that the Egyptians heard it, and the household of Pharaoh heard it. ³ And Joseph said to his brothers, "I am Joseph! Is my father still alive?" But his brothers could not answer him, for they were dismayed at his presence.*

⁴ So Joseph said to his brothers, "Come near to me, please." And they came near. And he said, "I am your brother, Joseph, whom you sold into Egypt. ⁵ And now do not be distressed or angry with yourselves because you sold me here, for God sent me before you to preserve life. ⁶ For the famine has been in the land these two years, and there are yet five years in which there will be neither plowing nor harvest. ⁷ And God sent me before you to preserve for you a remnant on earth, and to keep alive for you many survivors. ⁸ So it was not you who sent me here, but God. He has made me a father to Pharaoh, and lord of all his house and ruler over all the land of Egypt."

50 *¹⁵ When Joseph's brothers saw that their father was dead, they said, "It may be that Joseph will hate us and pay us back for all the evil that we did to him." ¹⁶ So they sent a message to Joseph, saying, "Your father gave this command before he died: ¹⁷ 'Say to Joseph, "Please forgive the transgression of your brothers and their sin, because they did evil to you."' And now, please forgive the transgression of the servants of the God of your father." Joseph wept when they spoke to him. ¹⁸ His brothers also came and fell down before him and said, "Behold, we are your servants." ¹⁹ But Joseph said to them, "Do not fear, for am I in the place of God? ²⁰ As for you, you meant evil against me, but God meant it for good, to bring it about that many people should be kept alive, as they are today."*

Luke 23:1-4, 20-26, 34-43 ESV

¹ Then the whole company of them arose and brought him before Pilate. ² And they began to accuse him, saying, "We found this man misleading our nation and forbidding us to give tribute to Caesar, and saying that he himself is Christ, a king." ³ And Pilate asked him, "Are you the King of the Jews?" And he answered him, "You have said so." ⁴ Then Pilate said to the chief priests and the crowds, "I find no guilt in this man." ⁵ But they were urgent, saying, "He stirs up the people, teaching throughout all Judea, from Galilee even to this place."

²⁰ Pilate addressed them once more, desiring to release Jesus, ²¹ but they kept shouting, "Crucify, crucify him!" ²² A third time he said to them, "Why? What evil has he done? I have found in him no guilt deserving death. I will therefore punish and release him." ²³ But they were urgent, demanding with loud cries that he should be crucified. And their voices prevailed. ²⁴ So Pilate decided that their demand should be granted. ²⁵ He released the man who had been thrown into prison for insurrection and murder, for whom they asked, but he delivered Jesus over to their will.

²⁶ And as they led him away, they seized one Simon of Cyrene, who was coming in from the country, and laid on him the cross, to carry it behind Jesus.

³⁴ And Jesus said, "Father, forgive them, for they know not what they do." And they cast lots to divide his garments. ³⁵ And the people stood by, watching, but the rulers scoffed at him, saying, "He saved others; let him save himself, if he is the Christ of God, his Chosen One!" ³⁶ The soldiers also mocked him, coming up and offering him sour wine ³⁷ and saying, "If you are the King of the Jews, save yourself!" ³⁸ There was also an inscription over him, "This is the King of the Jews."

³⁹ One of the criminals who were hanged railed at him, saying, "Are you not the Christ? Save yourself and us!" ⁴⁰ But the other rebuked him, saying, "Do you not fear God, since you are under the same sentence of condemnation? ⁴¹ And we indeed justly, for we are receiving the due reward of our deeds; but this man has done nothing wrong." ⁴² And he said, "Jesus, remember me when you come into your kingdom." ⁴³ And he said to him, "Truly, I say to you, today you will be with me in paradise."

☙

12.

Our Evil—God's Good

Genesis 45:1-8; 50:15-20
Luke 23:1-4, 20-26, 34-43 ESV

A dozen men in an ornate room. All others have been sent away. Ten of these men—full-grown, full-bearded men—clearly share a common heritage. They all wear the same simple garb of the shepherd. They all speak a language foreign to what is normally heard in this room.

The 10 men also share a secret—the secret of an old evil they committed whose memory will not go away. On this day, in this room, they share the worried look of men who sense danger but cannot see it.

Before them sits a young, clean-shaven man, whose dress and manner set him apart. For clothes, he wears the robe and ring of royalty. His manner conveys that calm assurance of one who knows himself to be the master of all he surveys. This is *his* room. He looks at these foreigners and sees their fear. It does not surprise him; he created it—on purpose.

There is a twelfth man in the room, but he is hardly more than a boy. He wears the clothing of the 10 who brought him, but if he were cleaned up a bit, he would bear an uncanny resemblance to the regal young man—the man they all fear.

What they do not know is that the stranger before them is *not* a stranger. He knows them—and he knows their secret. And he knows something else: He knows that the secret evil they did had in it the seed of God's salvation.

A dozen men alone together in an ornate room, and the stranger who is not a stranger has decided that it is time to speak.

"I am Joseph."

And with those words, the regal figure explodes the secret and turns the world and the future of all 12 of them upside down.

I am the brother you left for dead—and now I rule all of Egypt."

The 10 older men are terrified. They realize immediately they are in far greater jeopardy than they had imagined. They deserve the greatest punishment possible for what they did to Joseph their brother, and they know they are powerless to prevent the seemingly risen-from-the-dead Joseph from exacting his just revenge.

But in the years since their sin, they have come to acknowledge—at least among themselves—that what they did was sin. And more: they have come to grieve their evil and the pain it has caused their father and their family. And now to their amazement, because they have confessed their sin and demonstrated their remorse—the one they sinned against is willing—and able—to forgive them.

The brothers know that what they did to Joseph was evil. They know it, and Joseph knows it, and God knows it. But the miraculous thing is that in the all-knowing, all-powerful, redemptive hands of God, their evil has been turned into God's good. God has used their own sin to save them.

Now, fast forward some 16 centuries, and see their descendants conspiring to give another brother over to foreigners—to arrange His death. The chief priests and elders (the "older brothers" of their day) don't like what this impertinent Upstart has to tell them. And they don't appreciate His claiming a special relationship with their Father—their Heavenly Father.

So, like Joseph's brothers, they decide to do their "brother" Jesus in. In the process, He is stripped of His clothes, mocked and derided for His helplessness, and left for dead in a hole in the ground. It is evil, but they do what they do, and are prepared to live with their sin, because they think they have gotten away with murder.

But it doesn't work out that way, because there is a God Who is watching—and working out His will in and through the affairs of men—even through their evil deeds. Nothing that man has done remains "done" in the face of a God Who "un-does" and "re-does" all things according to His holy and eternal will. The evil we do does not remain forever—though the guilt of it may.

The evil does not remain as evil because God is not willing to allow evil to endure in the world that He is ever re-creating.

But what of those who do the evil? What of the brothers of Joseph—the countrymen of Jesus—and us?

Even if God redeems the evil deeds we have done, the deeds were evil when we did them, for we intended them so. And they would have remained so, except for God's grace redeeming them. We could never undo the evil we have done—and seldom would we have wanted to, even if we could, as long as we were not suffering the painful consequences our actions deserved.

But in order to redeem our evil, God first had to absorb it—to experience it ultimately as sin against Him. That's why the Psalmist would say to God, *"Against You, and You only, have I sinned."*[113] That's where every sin ends up: in the heart of God.

---

[113] Psalm 51:4, ESV.

And what is God's response to our sin against Him?

Well, contrary to the popular thinking, He does not condone it. He cannot—and remain a just God. This good God cannot condone our sins, but He can forgive us. He can and does include us in His glorious and gracious work of redemption. God redeems sin *and* sinner—if they will submit to Him.

The sin is easy. It always submits to the power and wisdom and will of God's redemptive work. Once done, a sinful act is inanimate—a lifeless thing, subject to God's acting upon it.

But the sinner is something else—some-*one* else—a being with a will of his own—able and inclined to oppose God both by doing evil, and then by resisting God's efforts to redeem him from what he has done—and from his desire to do it again. But there comes a day for everyone when resistance to God will end. That day may be delayed so long by the willful waywardness of the sinner that the possibility of redemption is gone.

The brothers of Joseph were afraid they had reached that point when they discovered that Joseph was not dead, but alive. They feared they had reached that point again with the death of their father Jacob. They were afraid that the victim of their sin was about to become the instrument of their punishment.

But it turns out that Joseph loved them so much—despite their sin against him—that he gave them time to repent. And when he saw that they had repented, he was able to exercise the forgiveness he was waiting and wanting to bestow.

❧

And in the same way on the Cross, Jesus would look at those who brought about His Crucifixion and pray to God for their forgiveness—based on their ignorance. Consider what an odd prayer it is: *"Father, forgive them, for they know not what they do."*

It would seem they knew exactly what they were doing. Pilate—a foreigner who didn't care a fig about their religion—tried repeatedly to talk them out of it, but they were determined to destroy this Brother they despised.

But Jesus was right about their not knowing, because they didn't understand that what they meant for evil, God meant for good. In the hands of God, their evil became good, just as the brothers' act of betrayal against Joseph so many years before, became, in the hands of God, the source of *their* salvation.

What is Jesus praying on the Cross?

He is asking God to delay judgment until those who brought about His death can see the good that God will bring out of it, and understand God's purpose in it, and repent, so that God's forgiveness can play out in their lives. Jesus prays that the good that God brings out of His death—an evil they brought about—will be so clearly and powerfully revealed, that God's redemption of their sin—and that of other sinners—through the Cross—will also eventually bring about the change of heart in them that enables God's redemption and salvation to work within them, too.

Joseph, who was the victim of his brothers' sin, has seen God redeem the evil done to him, and so he understands what they do not: they are forgiven—and through their contrition they enable themselves to receive that forgiveness. The debt of their sin has been cancelled and a new life lies before them.

And now, we stand like them, sinners of sins, facing the One against Whom we have sinned, certain of our guilt. If we are willing to confess it—we may know ourselves redeemed and restored by the One Who died because of—and for—our sins. We humble ourselves before the One Who was humbled by the sins of mankind, and Who before that, was humbled by His desire to serve His—*our*—Father,[114] the God Who sent Jesus ahead—as long before, He had sent Joseph—to endure the evil inflicted upon Him

---

[114] Philippians 2:7.

in order to prepare our way of salvation—to preserve us alive when we should have suffered what He suffered for us, instead.

Joseph was not God, but God was with him and turned the evil of his brothers into good.

Jesus was God, and God was with Him in a way that was like—but infinitely greater than—the way God was with Joseph. And the God Who was with and in—and *was*—Jesus has taken the sins, not just of 10 brothers, but of the whole world, and stands ready and able to give everyone in the world the means to live, not just through a few years of famine, but forever.

And for that reason, let us remember our sins, and turn them and ourselves over to God, so that like the sinner on the cross beside Jesus, we may ask to be—and know that we certainly are and will be—remembered by Him in the kingdom to which He came after His Crucifixion—that we are and will be forgiven of all our sins—our evil—that has, in Jesus, been transformed into God's good.

Isaiah 52:13—53:12 ESV

52 ¹³ *Behold, my servant shall act wisely;*
  he shall be high and lifted up,
  and shall be exalted.
¹⁴ *As many were astonished at you—*
  his appearance was so marred, beyond human semblance,
  and his form beyond that of the children of mankind—
¹⁵ *so shall he sprinkle many nations;*
  kings shall shut their mouths because of him;
for that which has not been told them they see,
  and that which they have not heard they understand.

53 ¹ *Who has believed what he has heard from us?*
  And to whom has the arm of the LORD been revealed?
² *For he grew up before him like a young plant,*
  and like a root out of dry ground;
he had no form or majesty that we should look at him,
  and no beauty that we should desire him.
³ *He was despised and rejected by men;*
  a man of sorrows, and acquainted with grief;
and as one from whom men hide their faces
  he was despised, and we esteemed him not.
⁴ *Surely he has borne our griefs*
  and carried our sorrows;
yet we esteemed him stricken,
  smitten by God, and afflicted.
⁵ *But he was pierced for our transgressions;*
  he was crushed for our iniquities;
upon him was the chastisement that brought us peace,
  and with his wounds we are healed.
⁶ *All we like sheep have gone astray;*
  we have turned—every one—to his own way;
  and the LORD has laid on him
  the iniquity of us all.

Good Friday

⁷ He was oppressed, and he was afflicted,
  yet he opened not his mouth;
like a lamb that is led to the slaughter,
  and like a sheep that before its shearers is silent,
so he opened not his mouth.
⁸ By oppression and judgment he was taken away;
  and as for his generation, who considered
that he was cut off out of the land of the living,
  stricken for the transgression of my people?
⁹ And they made his grave with the wicked
  and with a rich man in his death,
although he had done no violence,
  and there was no deceit in his mouth.
¹⁰ Yet it was the will of the LORD to crush him;
  he has put him to grief;
when his soul makes an offering for guilt,
  he shall see his offspring; he shall prolong his days;
the will of the LORD shall prosper in his hand.
¹¹ Out of the anguish of his soul he shall see and be satisfied;
by his knowledge shall the righteous one, my servant,
  make many to be accounted righteous,
  and he shall bear their iniquities.
¹² Therefore I will divide him a portion with the many,
  and he shall divide the spoil with the strong,
because he poured out his soul to death
  and was numbered with the transgressors;
yet he bore the sin of many,
  and makes intercession for the transgressors.

Matthew 27:22-31 ESV

²² Pilate said to them, "Then what shall I do with Jesus who is called Christ?" They all said, "Let him be crucified!" ²³ And he said, "Why, what evil has he done?" But they shouted all the more, "Let him be crucified!"

²⁴ So when Pilate saw that he was gaining nothing, but rather that a riot was beginning, he took water and washed his hands before the crowd, saying, "I am innocent of this man's blood; see to it yourselves." ²⁵ And all the people answered, "His blood be on us and on our children!" ²⁶ Then he released for them Barabbas, and having scourged Jesus, delivered him to be crucified.

²⁷ Then the soldiers of the governor took Jesus into the governor's headquarters, and they gathered the whole battalion before him. ²⁸ And they stripped him and put a scarlet robe on him, ²⁹ and twisting together a crown of thorns, they put it on his head and put a reed in his right hand. And kneeling before him, they mocked him, saying, "Hail, King of the Jews!" ³⁰ And they spit on him and took the reed and struck him on the head. ³¹ And when they had mocked him, they stripped him of the robe and put his own clothes on him and led him away to crucify him.

13.

Who *Is* This Guy?

Isaiah 52:13—53:12; Matthew 27:22-31 ESV

Today is a tough day to try and preach a sermon on the gospel of Jesus Christ. Kids are focused on the candy they will collect just a few days from now, and many adults are wondering whether the upcoming elections will provide the nation "tricks" or "treats," politically. We dress up the various candidates in our minds as superheroes or scary monsters—according to our political persuasions—and we are astonished that anybody could see them any other way.[115]

But today, for a few minutes if I can, I want to wean you away from the pull of politics and put before you a revelation that is, and always will be, far more important to you than any candidate or campaign that will ever seek your support. The revelation comes in several parts, like a picture whose different pieces come into focus separately, over time, until, finally, you can see enough to

---

[115] Confession: as this paragraph suggests, I preached this sermon, not on Good Friday, but on the Sunday before Halloween (and in an election year). Still, it is a sermon about the Crucifixion and—the costume character motif notwithstanding—may be helpful to those preparing to preach about the execution of Jesus, and meaningful to others who want to think more deeply about our Savior's sacrificial death. And so, I have "slipped it in" with sermons that *were* preached on Good Friday.

recognize the image for what it is. But until then, you may think what you see is something far removed from the true picture.

The first part of the picture is provided by the prophet Isaiah in the dark days of Exile. Isaiah painted the portrait of a mysterious figure—a servant of God who suffered as a substitute for God's people. At first, this servant of God looked like a scary monster—not because he was terrifying, but because he was so pathetic—because the signs of all the suffering he had endured showed for all to see. The only thing that was hidden from view was the fact that he was not a monster—that he was, in reality, God's superhero.

Nobody expected a superhero to be dressed up as a scary monster, and so they treated him like the monster they thought he was. Only later did people figure out who it was behind the hideous mask of suffering and shame, and why he wore—why *God* had him wear—the costume that so confused them.

Isaiah never named the name of that first Suffering Servant—though the people of Isaiah's time—God's people in exile—would surely have understood who the servant was when they finally saw how God had used him. They implied as much, in their confession about him. They knew who he was because they came to realize that his suffering was not God's punishment of him. It was God's punishment of *them*—placed, by God, on him.

※

Centuries passed. Isaiah and his generation died. History brought new nations and new generations into being. But the people of God endured, as did their sin and rebellion against God.

And so God sent another, even more significant, Servant. Whoever God sent as His suffering servant in the time of Isaiah, in the fullness of time, God sent His Son.[116] And this Son set aside

---

[116] Galatians 4:4.

the "perks" of His divinity in order to serve His Heavenly Father.[117]

The Bible says this Son, though He was God Himself,[118] was born of woman[119] and grew in wisdom and stature,[120] as all human beings must do.

The Bible says He humbled Himself and became obedient[121]—*learned* obedience from what He suffered.[122] He learned Who He was and what God had sent Him to do and how God intended for Him to do it. The Son of God found Who He was to be in the tailor-made model of the Suffering Servant of God—in the words of Isaiah. As He studied the holy scriptures throughout His life, He found that this special role fit Him to a "T."

God's glorious Son—the greatest "Superhero" of all time—would become the despised and rejected One, the One smitten and afflicted, pierced and crushed. He would be tortured and stripped, mocked and spit upon. Then, when His own mother would not have recognized Him and could not have stood to look at Him (but did), His enemies put Him to death in the cruelest and most humiliating way they could imagine. And the "good people" responsible for His death congratulated themselves for doing God a favor in getting rid of this monster.

But He was no monster. He was God's Superhero—God's glorious Champion—God's Suffering Servant—Who submitted Himself to the hideous mask of a monster in order to serve the redemptive will of God.

And it worked!

God said: *"See, my servant will act wisely; He will be raised and lifted up and highly exalted."*

---

[117] Philippians 2:6-7.
[118] John 1:1; Philippians 2:6; Colossians 1:15-19.
[119] Galatians 4:4.
[120] Luke 2:52.
[121] Philippians 2:8.
[122] Hebrews 5:8.

God said: *"After the suffering of his soul, he will see the light of life and be satisfied; because he poured out his life unto death, and was numbered with the transgressors, for he bore the sin of many, and made intercession for the transgressors."*

God said: *"This is my beloved Son, with whom I am well pleased."*[123]

And Peter preached: *"...we are witnesses of all that he did .... They put him to death by hanging him on a tree, but God raised him on the third day.... To him all the prophets bear witness that everyone who believes in him receives forgiveness of sins through his name."*[124]

The One that men thought was a monster was—is—God's Hero—for us. God subjected Jesus—His only-begotten Son—to all the suffering sinful men could devise. God gave Him up as a sacrifice for our sins—and made Him Someone some people could imagine a monster, so that the monster within each of us might be destroyed before it finally and completely destroys us.

We do not know whom Isaiah had in mind when God led him to portray someone as God's Suffering Servant in his day. But we know Whom God sent to suffer and die for us. And His is *"the name that is above every name,"* in heaven and on earth.[125] We know Jesus for the holy Hero He is.

But there are so many others who still despise Him and reject Him. More and more in our day—men and women who have heard the testimony of Isaiah and Peter and the followers of Jesus throughout history and in this generation, are happy to mock Jesus and spit on Him—figuratively, if not literally. They would strip Him of all dignity and subject Him to every humiliation they might hurl His way. "Yea, crucify Him! He's not worth our time!"

And we are aghast.

"Wait! Don't you people understand? This is Jesus! Jesus loves you. He gave His life for you. He suffered and bled and died on

---

[123] Matthew 3:17, ESV.
[124] Acts 10:39-40, 43, RSV.
[125] Philippians 2:9, ESV.

the Cross for your sins. *"The punishment that brought us peace was upon him, and by his wounds we are healed."*

Jesus Christ, the Suffering Servant of God, is our Savior, and we are astonished that anybody could see Him any other way. But until *we* believed, *"we esteemed him not."* And now, neither do they.

So, what do you do?

Well, the Halloween approach would be to sneak out and toilet paper their yards. The down-and-dirty political response would be to sneak out and steal their campaign signs. But the Suffering Servant of God says, *"Take up your cross and follow me."*[126] The Suffering Servant of God says, "Turn the other cheek and go the second mile and give away your cloak as well as your coat."[127]

The way Jesus wants you to deal with those who reject Him, ridicule Him, attack Him, is for you to become suffering servants of God for them, the way Jesus was for you.[128] Not that you can atone for their sins the way Jesus did for yours, but by enduring their criticism and abuse—without violence, without deceit, without responding in a spirit of anger or hostility—you point them most effectively to the One Who bore their transgressions and suffered—not what *He* deserved—but what *they* deserve, from God.

Remember that the Suffering Servant Song you read earlier from Isaiah was not just the affirmation of God that His Servant had served Him effectively through His suffering. It was also the confession of those for whom the Servant had suffered—those who finally came to realize what was going on all along and how wrong they had been about everything related to the Servant, and their own sinful lives.

We are called to be suffering servants like Jesus so that we may keep ever before those who are blind to God's redemptive,

---

[126] Luke 9:23.
[127] Matthew 5:39-41.
[128] Matthew 11:29.

sacrificial love in Jesus Christ, the picture that points to the greater reality—the ultimate truth—their only hope of salvation.[129]

All over our towns, committed people have put up signs to remind other people of the names they want them to know, in the hope they will make the same commitment. All over our TVs, we're seeing the faces and hearing the voices of various political heroes, because people have invested in the effort to win "the undecided" to them.

You and I wear the face of Jesus for—and speak His words to—an indifferent and increasingly hostile world. We do these things as a sign to those who are rejecting Him now, in the hope that one day they will open the eyes of their hearts to see Him, and hear with clarity and conviction the good news of salvation made possible for them through the suffering of the One Who endured the Cross—and, even now, endures their rejection.

We do not know who will yet "cast their vote" for Jesus Christ. We do not know what it will take to get any particular person to come over to the side of the Savior. But we do know what He suffered for us, and that He suffered the same for everyone, friend and foe alike, in obedience to God's will, in the service of God's love.

Someday, everyone will see the truth—everyone will know that the One Who suffered for them was the Suffering Servant of God. Let us hope and pray, and live like Christ, so that, for as many as possible, that day will not come too late.

---

[129] Acts 4:12.

1 Peter 2:21-24 ESV

²¹ For to this you have been called, because Christ also suffered for you, leaving you an example, so that you might follow in his steps. ²² He committed no sin, neither was deceit found in his mouth. ²³ When he was reviled, he did not revile in return; when he suffered, he did not threaten, but continued entrusting himself to him who judges justly. ²⁴ He himself bore our sins in his body on the tree, that we might die to sin and live to righteousness. By his wounds you have been healed.

Matthew 27:33-54 ESV

³³ And when they came to a place called Golgotha (which means Place of a Skull), ³⁴ they offered [Jesus] wine to drink, mixed with gall, but when he tasted it, he would not drink it. ³⁵ And when they had crucified him, they divided his garments among them by casting lots. ³⁶ Then they sat down and kept watch over him there. ³⁷ And over his head they put the charge against him, which read, "This is Jesus, the King of the Jews." ³⁸ Then two robbers were crucified with him, one on the right and one on the left. ³⁹ And those who passed by derided him, wagging their heads ⁴⁰ and saying, "You who would destroy the temple and rebuild it in three days, save yourself! If you are the Son of God, come down from the cross." ⁴¹ So also the chief priests, with the scribes and elders, mocked him, saying, ⁴² "He saved others; he cannot save himself. He is the King of Israel; let him come down now from the cross, and we will believe in him. ⁴³ He trusts in God; let God deliver him now, if he desires him. For he said, 'I am the Son of God.'" ⁴⁴ And the robbers who were crucified with him also reviled him in the same way.

⁴⁵ Now from the sixth hour there was darkness over all the land until the ninth hour. ⁴⁶ And about the ninth hour Jesus cried out with a loud voice, saying, "Eli, Eli, lema sabachthani?" that is, "My God, my God, why have you forsaken me?" ⁴⁷ And some of the bystanders, hearing it, said, "This man is calling Elijah." ⁴⁸ And one of them at once ran and took a sponge, filled it with sour wine, and put it on a reed and gave it to him to drink. ⁴⁹ But the

others said, "Wait, let us see whether Elijah will come to save him." ⁵⁰ And Jesus cried out again with a loud voice and yielded up his spirit.

⁵¹ And behold, the curtain of the temple was torn in two, from top to bottom. And the earth shook, and the rocks were split. ⁵² The tombs also were opened. And many bodies of the saints who had fallen asleep were raised, ⁵³ and coming out of the tombs after his resurrection they went into the holy city and appeared to many. ⁵⁴ When the centurion and those who were with him, keeping watch over Jesus, saw the earthquake and what took place, they were filled with awe and said, "Truly this was the Son of God!"

14.

This is Jesus

1 Peter 2:21-24; Matthew 27:33-54 ESV

Last Sunday, we walked with Jesus into the city of Jerusalem and watched Him as He traveled in triumph. Today, we walk with Him—behind Him—out of the city and up a nearby hill called "Golgotha" or "Calvary," to watch Him die as He had predicted He would. And with our hearts breaking, we listen to what He says, and watch what He does, and discover, finally, Who He truly is.

❧❧

It is an awful, horrible scene: the torture of these men, displayed in public to humiliate them, and dragged out, seemingly forever, to extend their agony beyond endurance. None of the modern, make-believe horrors on TV or the movie screens can compete with the reality of this.

But what is the reality of "this"? And Who is this Man dying on the middle cross, really?

There are those who thought they knew—His disciples. But now their certainty is shattered by what they see. There are others—many others—who are certain they know Who He is, but are absolutely wrong, because they cannot and will not see the truth.

And there are those who don't care one way or the other when they nail Him to the tree. But they will be forced to care by what they see and hear as the ungodly process proceeds.

There is a sign, of course, nailed to the cross above His head, telling everybody Who He is: *"This is Jesus, the king of the Jews."*

"This is Jesus."

That part's true. The rest is a joke—a cynical slap by a magistrate at the mob that has out-maneuvered him. They get their Roman ruler to do what they want when he doesn't want to and knows he shouldn't. And then, for spite, he inserts a little insult in the script they have written for him.

And they "get" it: "Don't say, 'He is the king of the Jews!'"[130]

"What I have written I have written," he replies,[131] as though nobody can change his mind or affect his actions, when that's exactly what they've done.

When the day began, Pilate didn't know Jesus from jelly, but now he knows Who Jesus is. But he doesn't really, because for Pilate, the royal title is just a ruse to rile up the Jews who manipulated him into murdering an innocent Man—the most innocent Man in all the world.

"This is Jesus, the king of the Jews," except most of the Jews hanging around Jesus right now aren't buying it. He's no king in their eyes. Kings don't die on crosses, and anyway, they've already gone on record that they *"have no king but Caesar!"*[132]

This is Jesus, all right, but He wasn't saying what they wanted to hear their king say, and He wasn't doing what they thought their king would do to prove He *was* their king. And so the rabble rousers among them deride Him and taunt Him, just for the fun of it. The poor wretches dying on either side of Him yell at Him, too, but perhaps they can be excused because they are out of their

---

[130] John 19:21, ESV.
[131] John 19:22, ESV.
[132] John 19:15, ESV.

minds with the pain of their ordeal and are probably yelling at everyone in sight.

The most interesting bunch of disbelievers are those who don't bother directing their abuse at Jesus. The religious leaders are there making sure that all the onlookers understand that this Jesus is not Who He and His disciples said He was.

"He said He was the Son of God. If He is, He ought to come down. If He came down off that cross right now, we would believe. But there He hangs. Doesn't look much like a king to us"—which is just what they had in mind when they had Him crucified: Kill the Man; kill His message.

As the sign says, *"This is Jesus..."* This poor, wretched, barely-recognizable Man, nailed to a cross, dying in agony to the delight of His enemies, is Jesus. I say "barely recognizable," because He is recognized, despite everything the Roman authorities have done to Him and all the religious leaders are saying about Him. One of the men dying in agony beside Him will recognize Jesus and pray to Him for his future: *"Jesus, remember me when You come into Your kingdom."*[133] This is Jesus, a hopeless man's Hope.

And when darkness above and earthquakes below accompany the death of this Jesus, even His executioners come out of their callous complacency to call Him "the Son of God."

This is Jesus, Divinity dying a sinner's death and melting some of the hardest of hearts in the process.

More than all the words He ever spoke—more than all the miracles He ever worked—*this* is Jesus. The sign written in derision turns out to be right: *"This is Jesus"*—and despite all odds and all arguments to the contrary, He *is "the king of the Jews"*—and of the Gentiles—and of all the world—for all time, past, present and future. And He is never more the King, and never more deserving of our allegiance, than when He is hanging upon that cross and dying for our sins.

---

[133] Luke 23:39-42, ESV.

The crown of thorns is, truly, the crown of a King—the King of all kings. The Cross is His throne and the Crucifixion His coronation. They said He was not a king because He could not avoid a cross. He was and is *the* King because He *would* not avoid it. He took up His Cross, voluntarily, and gave up His life upon it, completely, because that was what this King was commissioned by God to do.

This is Jesus—not, first of all, inspiring Teacher—not miraculous Healer or mighty Worker of wonders—as wonderful as all those aspects of His identity are. This is Jesus, *"the Lamb of God, Who takes away the sins of the world."*[134]

Jesus on the Cross dying is the one act of His that validates all the others. Without this, the rest of Jesus is nothing. Because of it, Jesus is everything—everything God sent Him to be—everything you and I and everyone else need Him to be.

Without this—this holy and complete, atoning sacrifice—there is no reason for the Resurrection—and no point in your faith. But because we are not without it, everything He said and did is forever true—and truly powerful.

❦

Funny thing, though: Jesus has just as many mockers and deriders and revilers today as He had on the day He died on the Cross—more, really, even though there *was* a Resurrection and countless confirmations down through the centuries of the faith of His followers who now number in the millions and cover the globe.

But Jesus is still a favorite target of those who are hurting: "Jesus, why don't You make my pain and sorrow go away? Why did you let this happen to me?"

But *"when He suffered, He did not threaten."* And neither do we. We pray that, like the thief beside Him, those who suffer will see

---

[134] John 1:29, ESV.

that Jesus suffers with them, and that their hostility will turn to hope—in Him.

Jesus is still a favorite target of those who like to make fun of the seemingly helpless or those they know will not strike back. But they don't know Jesus. They misunderstand the reason He did not revile when He was reviled. They ignore the risk they run with the One Who judges justly—the One to Whom Jesus continued to entrust Himself, even on the Cross.

We live in an age and a culture in which our faith in Jesus is ridiculed. Don't be bothered by that. As Peter wrote, *"Christ also suffered for you, leaving you an example, so that you might follow in his steps."*

This is Jesus and those who do not recognize Him will discover that the last laugh will be on them, if you can call it that, when the One Who judges justly judges them.

And then, there are those, even today, for whom the destruction of the message of Jesus and the undermining of His saving influence in our lives is deadly serious business. They know Who they're dealing with and why they want to recreate the crucifixion of everything to do with Jesus. They are powerful. They are persuasive. They are persistent. And they have led many millions astray.

But the truth is still the truth, today as then: *"He bore our sins in his body on the tree, that we might die to sin and live to righteousness. By his wounds you have been healed."*

It was a horrible thing they did to Jesus when they nailed Him to the Cross. Yet, in dying on that cross, an innocent Man, sent and sentenced to suffer, surrounded by those who took pleasure in His pain, Jesus did a beautiful thing for us—and for all who believe that *this*—this *Jesus*—*is* the King of kings, the Son of God.

Hanging Out with Jesus

Luke 23:32-43 ESV

³² Two others, who were criminals, were led away to be put to death with him. ³³ And when they came to the place that is called The Skull, there they crucified [Jesus], and the criminals, one on his right and one on his left. ³⁴ And Jesus said, "Father, forgive them, for they know not what they do." And they cast lots to divide his garments. ³⁵ And the people stood by, watching, but the rulers scoffed at him, saying, "He saved others; let him save himself, if he is the Christ of God, his Chosen One!" ³⁶ The soldiers also mocked him, coming up and offering him sour wine ³⁷ and saying, "If you are the King of the Jews, save yourself!" ³⁸ There was also an inscription over him, "This is the King of the Jews."

³⁹ One of the criminals who were hanged railed at him, saying, "Are you not the Christ? Save yourself and us!" ⁴⁰ But the other rebuked him, saying, "Do you not fear God, since you are under the same sentence of condemnation? ⁴¹ And we indeed justly, for we are receiving the due reward of our deeds; but this man has done nothing wrong." ⁴² And he said, "Jesus, remember me when you come into your kingdom." ⁴³ And he said to him, "Truly, I say to you, today you will be with me in Paradise."

15.

Hanging Out with Jesus

Luke 23:32-43 ESV

It was a busy place, that skull-shaped hill outside Jerusalem, on that Friday before Passover. Thousands of people were pouring into the holy city of God, surging up the road that ran past that hideous hill covered with crosses. Pilgrims from all over the world had but hours to get inside the city gates and settle in before the sun went down and the Passover Sabbath began. There was no time to pause and consider the poor wretches hanging on the crosses who had but hours to live (if you could call it that) before the darkness of merciful death settled in upon them.

Countless men, women and children were coming to Jerusalem to make their way up the Temple Mount to get close to their God, not knowing that they would never be closer to God than when they passed under the shadow of the men hanging on the crosses on that hill outside the city.

And if the endless parade of pilgrims paid no attention to the crosses—or the men hanging on them—or to any of the other people crowding around the crosses—the people on the hill—on Calvary—were paying no attention to the pilgrims, either. Some of the people on the hill—a few men and all the women—were suffering as much emotional agony as the crucified were suffering physically. As for the rest, there were Roman soldiers indifferently doing their duty. There were the ghoulish gawkers, the kind who gather just to witness cruelty. And there were religious and political leaders who had come out to satisfy themselves that one particular Person would die upon a cross that day, just as they had arranged.

And high above the pilgrims—head and shoulders above everybody else on that grizzly hill—were the three men hanging on the crosses: two thieves—and the Savior of the world.

༄༅༅

For all the world, the three looked just alike, stripped of their clothes and their last shred of dignity—tortured beyond imagination—with each breath, struggling to live and desperate to die.

But they weren't the same—these three—and they all three knew it. The thieves were more like the crowd at their feet, and the pilgrims on the road, than they were like the Man hanging between them—with them.

They were thieves. They were being crucified because they were *caught* thieves. They deserved to be where they were. And truth be told, a lot of other people deserved to be hanging from crosses more than the Man nailed to the cross between them. Every person who ever lived deserved to be hanging there more than He did.

But there, between two thieves, dying on a Roman cross, hung Jesus of Nazareth, King of the Jews, Son of the Living God, Savior of the world—as unlike the two thieves who hung with Him as a man or God could be—and yet, enough like them and us that He *could* die with them—and *for* them—which was exactly why He was there: God Incarnate dying for the sins of the world—dying for sinners hanging on crosses—and those who should be.

They knew He was different—these two thieves—just like everybody on the ground knew. But knowing He was different didn't bring the same response—from the witnesses on the hill—

Good Friday

or even from the two seemingly similar thieves on their crosses. For all their similarities, the two thieves turned out to be fundamentally—and forever—different from each other.

Both thieves needed to be saved—and they knew it. Crucifixion focuses your mind rather effectively on what you need most. Both desperately wanted to be saved. The difference was that one thief believed Jesus could do the saving; the other thief didn't. Two great needs. One believing heart.

One thief summed up all the cynicism and bitterness of the unbelieving of this world, past and present, by taunting Jesus: "If You really are the Christ, save Yourself—*and us.*" In other words: "If You are really the Ruler of all Creation, let us rule You. Do what we tell You to do. Do what we want done. We don't believe You can, but we really, desperately, want and need *someone* to do for us what You say *You* can do. We just know that "someone" isn't *You*. We don't believe You can save us because You're not doing it the way we think it should be done—the want we want it to be done. You're just like us, Jesus. You're hanging on a cross right here beside us. That's not what we want. We want somebody to save us."

But how can you be saved, if you don't believe in the Savior's ability to save?

ॐ

And that's how they're different, these two thieves on their crosses—these two miserable wretches dying on either side of Jesus. One attacks Jesus in his dis-belief. The other believes—believes that, even on their crosses, Jesus can save him. And he asks Jesus to give him what the other thief doubts that Jesus has the power to give.

"*If* You are the Christ, save Yourself—and *me!*" "*If* You are…," says the first thief.

How different, his partner in crime: "Jesus, *because* You are the Christ, remember me. I know I'm a sinner who deserves what I'm getting. Save me, I pray, *despite* what I deserve."

The believing thief sees his last chance and jumps at it (figuratively speaking). The un-believing thief will not make that leap of faith—even though it's the only leap he has left, nailed to a cross while his life ebbs away.

❧

The truth is: we're all thieves, really—crooks, criminals, rebels, sinners. We steal from God's goodness everyday—or try to—trying to be God for ourselves, thinking that it is as easy and natural for us to be gods as it was for God to become man. And if you haven't been crucified for it yet—if you haven't suffered the full penalty for your sins yet—it's only because you haven't been caught or made to pay—yet. But you will be. We all will, sooner or later—unless….

The question is: when it's your turn to hang with Jesus, will you join the world in ridicule and disbelief, throwing your last chance for salvation away in a dazzling display of sophisticated stupidity? Or will you throw yourself on the mercy of the One Man Whose hanging on a cross really did make it possible for you to be saved?

❧

"If You are the Christ, save Yourself!" one thief and so many others yelled at Jesus.

But if You are the Christ, the last thing in the world You want to do is save *Yourself*—especially when You've gotten this far.

If You are the Christ, You are hanging on the Cross, not because powerful people put You there, but because Almighty God, Your Heavenly Father, *sent* You there.

The greatest miracle that could happen on that hill outside Jerusalem on that Friday before Passover would not be for the Man on the middle cross to save Himself by somehow coming down from it after His executioners had so capably nailed Him up on it. The greatest miracle is going to be for Him to continue to hang on that cross until He dies there to save all the sinners of the world—*by* His dying there. All the sinners in the world: the sinners on the other two crosses—and the sinners assembled on that hill below Him—and the sinners making their way into Jerusalem on the pilgrim's road beside Him—and you and me: saved, if we believe He can do it—which He can, even while He is hanging on a cross.

"Remember me, when you come into your kingdom!" one of the thieves said. No *"ifs."* No uncertainty—in spite of the fact that this thief is a dying man hanging on a cross, praying to another dying Man Who happens to be hanging on the cross next to him.

And miracle of miracles, by asking *this* Man—hanging—dying—on a cross—for what he needs most, a guilty sinner gets just that: salvation—the promise of paradise. And in the process, he gets closer to God than any pilgrim who ever went looking for God anywhere else. And so do we.

Remember me, Crucified Lord, when You come into Your kingdom.

John 19:1-22, 28-34 NRSV

¹ Then Pilate took Jesus and had him flogged. ² And the soldiers wove a crown of thorns and put it on his head, and they dressed him in a purple robe. ³ They kept coming up to him, saying, "Hail, King of the Jews!" and striking him on the face. ⁴ Pilate went out again and said to them, "Look, I am bringing him out to you to let you know that I find no case against him." ⁵ So Jesus came out, wearing the crown of thorns and the purple robe. Pilate said to them, "Here is the man!" ⁶ When the chief priests and the police saw him, they shouted, "Crucify him! Crucify him!" Pilate said to them, "Take him yourselves and crucify him; I find no case against him." ⁷ The Jews answered him, "We have a law, and according to that law he ought to die because he has claimed to be the Son of God."

⁸ Now when Pilate heard this, he was more afraid than ever. ⁹ He entered his headquarters again and asked Jesus, "Where are you from?" But Jesus gave him no answer. ¹⁰ Pilate therefore said to him, "Do you refuse to speak to me? Do you not know that I have power to release you, and power to crucify you?" ¹¹ Jesus answered him, "You would have no power over me unless it had been given you from above; therefore the one who handed me over to you is guilty of a greater sin." ¹² From then on Pilate tried to release him, but the Jews cried out, "If you release this man, you are no friend of the emperor. Everyone who claims to be a king sets himself against the emperor."

¹³ When Pilate heard these words, he brought Jesus outside and sat on the judge's bench at a place called The Stone Pavement, or in Hebrew Gabbatha. ¹⁴ Now it was the day of Preparation for the Passover; and it was about noon. He said to the Jews, "Here is your King!" ¹⁵ They cried out, "Away with him! Away with him! Crucify him!" Pilate asked them, "Shall I crucify your King?" The chief priests answered, "We have no king but the emperor." ¹⁶ Then he handed him over to them to be crucified.

So they took Jesus; ¹⁷ and carrying the cross by himself, he went out to what is called The Place of the Skull, which in Hebrew is called Golgotha. ¹⁸ There they crucified him, and with him two others, one on either side, with Jesus between them. ¹⁹ Pilate also had an inscription written and put on the cross. It read, "Jesus of Nazareth, the King of the Jews." ²⁰ Many of the Jews read this inscription, because the place where Jesus was crucified was near the city; and it was written in Hebrew, in Latin, and in Greek. ²¹ Then the chief priests of the Jews said to Pilate, "Do not write, 'The King of the Jews,' but, 'This man said, I am King of the Jews.'" ²² Pilate answered, "What I have written I have written."

²⁸ After this, when Jesus knew that all was now finished, he said (in order to fulfill the scripture), "I am thirsty." ²⁹ A jar full of sour wine was standing there. So they put a sponge full of the wine on a branch of hyssop and held it to his mouth. ³⁰ When Jesus had received the wine, he said, "It is finished." Then he bowed his head and gave up his spirit.

³¹ Since it was the day of Preparation, the Jews did not want the bodies left on the cross during the Sabbath, especially because that Sabbath was a day of great solemnity. So they asked Pilate to have the legs of the crucified men broken and the bodies removed. ³² Then the soldiers came and broke the legs of the first and of the other who had been crucified with him. ³³ But when they came to Jesus and saw that he was already dead, they did not break his legs. ³⁴ Instead, one of the soldiers pierced his side with a spear, and at once blood and water came out. ³⁵ (He who saw this has testified so that you also may believe. His testimony is true, and he knows that he tells the truth.) ³⁶ These things occurred so that the scripture might be fulfilled, "None of his bones shall be broken." ³⁷ And again another passage of scripture says, "They will look on the one whom they have pierced."

³⁸ After these things, Joseph of Arimathea, who was a disciple of Jesus, though a secret one because of his fear of the Jews, asked Pilate to let him take away the body of Jesus. Pilate gave him permission; so he came and removed his body. ³⁹ Nicodemus, who had at first come to Jesus by night, also came, bringing a mixture of myrrh and aloes, weighing about a hundred pounds. ⁴⁰ They took the body of Jesus and wrapped it with the spices in linen cloths, according to the burial custom of the Jews. ⁴¹ Now there was a garden in the place where he was crucified, and in the garden there was a new tomb in which no one had ever been laid. ⁴² And so, because it was the Jewish day of Preparation, and the tomb was nearby, they laid Jesus there.

☙❧

16.

What Does It Take...?

John 19:1-22, 28-34 NRSV

What does it take to break your heart?

Perhaps the gaunt and haunting faces of wretched, starving children, or the bloody carnage of a terrorist bomb. Or does it take something more personal, like the destruction of a marriage or the death of someone who is very dear?

Does the Crucifixion—the sight and sound of Jesus being nailed to the Cross—break your heart? Can you look and listen as this Man—this particular Man, already taunted and tortured—is hammered on to wood and hung up to die? Does it break your heart?

It should. It's intended to. And there's nothing shameful in admitting it—no matter how big and strong you think you are. It broke God's heart.

The agony and revulsion you feel as you look upon Jesus being crucified is like the agony and revulsion God the Father feels as the spikes are driven into the body of His only-begotten Son and the Word Who became flesh struggles to breathe when each breath only prolongs His pain.

Jesus assured His disciples, *"I and the Father are one."*[135]

And so you know that the suffering of Jesus is the suffering of God Himself. What parent can endure the suffering of a beloved child? And yet God does, on that Good Friday. God endures the agony of His Son Jesus Christ, scourged and stripped of all human hope or dignity. God endures the sight—the experience—with broken heart—because God is witness to the death of the One He holds most dear.

The Crucifixion broke God's heart. He could not—or would not, if you like—look upon the suffering of His holy Son. There are, of course, those who suggest that God turned away from the scene unfolding on Calvary for another reason: because of what Jesus had become morally as the substitute for all the sin of all humanity.

They point to Paul's words that *"[God] made him to be sin..."*[136] as the basis for suggesting that God would not look upon the concentrated evil of the world now borne by Jesus as the sacrificial Lamb of God. Certainly, Jesus felt a sense of divine abandonment, whatever the cause: *"My God, my God, why have you forsaken me?"*[137] But moral revulsion is not incompatible with a broken heart.

It was this same God Who claimed the children of Israel as His beloved ones. The prophet Hosea recorded the broken heart of God centuries before that dark Friday at Calvary:

> *"When Israel was a child, I loved him*
> *and out of Egypt I called My son.*
> [But] *the more I called them,*
> *the more they went from Me...."* [138]

And yet even as He pronounced His disgust with their sin and His judgment upon them, God spoke His heart in the very next breath:

---

[135] John 10:30, ESV.
[136] 2 Corinthians 5:21, ESV.
[137] Matthew 27:46, ESV, quoting Psalm 22:1.
[138] Hosea 11:1-2, RSV.

"How can I give you up...!
How can I hand you over, O Israel!"[139]

God has had a heart-breaking relationship with sinful humanity ever since the first human committed the first sin.[140] Though the crucifixion of His only begotten Son Jesus breaks God's heart, it was God's idea—and His will—that Jesus should be crucified.

This crucifixion—this gory expression of human sin—is also a glorious expression of God's love. It is the culmination of God's plan to do something permanently redemptive about the sin that breaks God's heart. "For our sake [God] made him who knew no sin to be sin, so that in him we might become the righteousness of God."[141]

The Crucifixion broke God's heart just like the sin in every human life broke God's heart every day before the Crucifixion.

And because Jesus and the Father were One, the human sin that broke God's heart also broke the heart of Jesus. That's why, before they led Jesus out of Jerusalem to crucify Him, He had looked over into Jerusalem and cried out to them, "O Jerusalem, Jerusalem, you who kill the prophets and stone those sent to you, how often I have longed to gather your children together, as a hen gathers her chicks under her wings, but you were not willing."[142]

The horror of the Crucifixion, like the human sin that required it, was enough to break God's heart. The question is: "Is it enough to break yours?"

❧

Don't misunderstand: God's purpose in sending Jesus to the Cross was not to make us sinners sad. In the Crucifixion, God fulfilled the plan He put in motion with the confrontation of Adam and Eve in the Garden.[143] God did what He needed to do in the

---

[139] Hosea 11:8, RSV.
[140] Genesis 3.
[141] 2 Corinthians 5:21, ESV.
[142] Matthew 23:37, NIV.
[143] Again, Genesis 3.

Crucifixion of Jesus. Whatever you feel, there's still all that business of atoning sacrifice and propitiation for sin—the miraculous business of God that makes our salvation possible, despite our sin.

But until our hearts are broken—until the hardness of sin that holds our hearts and lives captive is shattered—we cannot receive the benefit of the heart-wrenching suffering Jesus endured—for us. It is not enough that our hearts are broken—even by the horrors of the Lord's Crucifixion.

Our feelings do not overcome the guilt of our sin—even if we feel what we should. Our sin must be atoned for, permanently and properly, which only the Crucifixion can do.

But if the suffering of Jesus—if His shed Blood and sacrificial death—do not break your heart, the salvation that has been won for you at such great price upon the Cross will have nowhere to go in your life. It *must* break your heart!

"Oh, it did break my heart! I remember I was so moved at one time in my life by the Crucifixion that I just opened up to God. Yes, the Crucifixion broke my heart."

Good! And does it still?

When you look upon your Savior, high and lifted up, broken and bleeding—now—today—does the image so familiar still reach into your heart and rip it open to God? Does the Crucifixion keep your heart conditioned like God's: grieving over sin and humbled by the sacrifice that overcomes all sin?

༺❦༻

What does it take to break your heart?

We began with that question, but let's not end with it. As you humble yourself, broken in heart before the Savior's broken Body, you are in the proper position to ask another and equally important question: "What does it take to mend your soul?"

You see, breaking your heart is not the purpose of the Crucifixion; but it is the essential preparation for the miracle that is the Crucifixion's purpose. When your heart is broken, your soul can be mended.

When you gaze upon the God-awful image of Jesus, the suffering Servant of God, your open heart becomes the avenue for the atoning, redeeming, saving grace of this awesome God to flow into your soul—even as His Blood flows out of His Body—and repair the damage sin has done in you.

It is a heartbreaking thing to watch and listen as Jesus is crucified—heartbreaking for God, and, I pray, heartbreaking for you. But if hearts are broken in heaven and on earth by the agonizing death of the God Who became Man, see as well that the relationship between you and God that sin had severed is, in this sorrow, restored.

"Behold the Man!" said Pilate after he had tortured Jesus. What he meant was, "Behold what His enemies and my guards have done to Him. Behold what I am *going* to do to Him."

Pilate speaks to assuage his own conscience and perhaps to shift the blame for what he knows is a failure of human justice. But Pilate, like everybody else in John's Gospel, speaks the words of God without knowing it.

"Behold the Man" Who was sent by God the Father to die for your sins—Who by His suffering and death on the Cross will do what God was willing to endure His own heartbreak to accomplish: the end of God's heartbreak over the sin-broken condition of your soul.

Look at that Cross! Behold the Man, Jesus Christ crucified! It's enough to break your heart—and mend your soul forever.

Learning Obedience

Hebrews 5:1-10 NRSV

¹ Every high priest chosen from among mortals is put in charge of things pertaining to God on their behalf, to offer gifts and sacrifices for sins. ² He is able to deal gently with the ignorant and wayward, since he himself is subject to weakness; ³ and because of this he must offer sacrifice for his own sins as well as for those of the people. ⁴ And one does not presume to take this honor, but takes it only when called by God, just as Aaron was.

⁵ So also Christ did not glorify himself in becoming a high priest, but was appointed by the one who said to him,
> *"You are my Son,*
>> *today I have begotten you";*

⁶ as he says also in another place,
> *"You are a priest forever,*
>> *according to the order of Melchizedek."*

⁷ In the days of his flesh, Jesus offered up prayers and supplications, with loud cries and tears, to the one who was able to save him from death, and he was heard because of his reverent submission. ⁸ Although he was a Son, he learned obedience through what he suffered; ⁹ and having been made perfect, he became the source of eternal salvation for all who obey him, ¹⁰ having been designated by God a high priest according to the order of Melchizedek.

17.

Learning Obedience

Hebrews 5:1-10 NRSV

You're going to have to stay with me today. We've got heavy stuff to talk about. No jokes—no laughter—just Hebrews, Chapter 5. And for our purposes, just two verses—8 and 9: *"Though being a Son, Jesus learned, from the things he suffered, obedience. And being perfected, he became, to all who are obeying him, the source of eternal salvation."*

Now it's hard to imagine Jesus needing to learn *anything*. Sure, Luke says, *"Jesus increased in wisdom"* (among other things) as He was growing up.[144] But by the time He was grown and about His ministry, Jesus was the One doing the teaching. What did He have to learn?

Certainly not obedience. Nobody was more committed to obedience than Jesus. It wasn't like He needed help getting from disobedience to obedience, or from a little obedience to more obedience. Still, it says Jesus learned obedience through what He suffered.

Let's consider this business of obedience. It's easy to be obedient when you are directed to do something you want to do anyway. It's still relatively easy to obey when you are told to do

---

[144] Luke 2:52, NRSV.

something you're not opposed to doing, even if you don't have a desire to do it already.

But obedience takes on a different meaning when you're given an assignment you would never do unless you were told to. And when you're told to do the last thing in the world you would want to do, your obedience teaches you something you could not learn any other way. You learn what obedience *means*. In His suffering, Jesus learned what His commitment to obedience meant in a way no theoretical understanding could convey.

And because of His obedience, something happened that would never have happened if He had not been completely obedient. Jesus became the Source or Cause of eternal salvation, not based on His obedience, but on His suffering, suffering that He would not have endured if He had wavered in His obedience to God under the fear or the pain of what He was to suffer.

And the culmination of that suffering was His death on the Cross. The Crucifixion completed a life that experienced all the temptations known to man—all the temptation, and yet none of the sin. Jesus was living a perfect life every day of His life, but it wasn't until His life was over—which it wasn't until Calvary—it wasn't until then that He was *perfected* as the Source of our salvation.

In the completion of the suffering He obediently accepted, Jesus achieved our salvation…

…*if*, that is to say, *we* are being obedient to *Him*. The Book of Hebrews is written to people who are learning that obedience to Jesus requires *them* to suffer, too. They are learning what Christian obedience means in terms of suffering—and they don't like it.

But they must also learn that there is no salvation without that suffering because there is no salvation without the obedience of Jesus to the Father and our obedience to Jesus. Jesus learned that, even being the Son of God, His commitment to obedience to God His Father still required great suffering.

Jesus is now the perfected Son of God Who has made us perfectly acceptable *to* God—*through* His suffering. Jesus has made us sons and daughters of God—but only if we are obeying Him—following Him—trusting in Him—even in the midst of suffering.

But an interesting thing happens when you continue to obey Jesus in spite of the suffering such obedience entails. You learn the *meaning* of *your* obedience. Your commitment to obedience moves from theoretical to experiential. You understand your suffering within the framework of your salvation. You see *your* suffering in the light of *His* suffering.

We learn obedience from Him as we experience suffering—and our eternal salvation—in Him.

The Empty God

Philippians 2:2-11 ESV

²...complete my joy by being of the same mind, having the same love, being in full accord and of one mind. ³ Do nothing from selfish ambition or conceit, but in humility count others more significant than yourselves. ⁴ Let each of you look not only to his own interests, but also to the interests of others. ⁵ Have this mind among yourselves, which is yours in Christ Jesus, ⁶ who, though he was in the form of God, did not count equality with God a thing to be grasped, ⁷ but emptied himself, by taking the form of a servant, being born in the likeness of men. ⁸ And being found in human form, he humbled himself by becoming obedient to the point of death, even death on a cross. ⁹ Therefore God has highly exalted him and bestowed on him the name that is above every name, ¹⁰ so that at the name of Jesus every knee should bow, in heaven and on earth and under the earth, ¹¹ and every tongue confess that Jesus Christ is Lord, to the glory of God the Father.

18.

The Empty God

Philippians 2:2-11 ESV

The Bible begins with a profound and primal truth: *"In the beginning, God created the heavens and the earth. And the earth was without form, and void"*—or "empty."[145]

The Gospel of John begins with an equally profound revelation: *"In the beginning was the Word, and the Word was with God, and the Word was God.... And the Word was made flesh, and dwelt among us...."*[146]

Creation and New Creation.

And Paul adds to the revelation of this New Creation in the second chapter of his Philippian letter, the text for today. And if he had put it in the literary form of the beginning verses of Genesis and John, he might have said, "In the new beginning, God designated a Savior from the heavens for the earth, and the Savior was God, and this time, it was the God Who would save the world Who was without form and void"—a simple, single human cell, to begin with—placed, by the will of God and nothing else, in a virgin's womb.

---

[145] Genesis 1:1-2, KJV.
[146] John 1:1, 14, KJV.

"Christ Jesus," Paul says, "...was in the form of God...." He was the equal of God. In Colossians, Christ is called "the image of...God..." in Whom "all the fullness of God was pleased to dwell."[147]

We're talking about God here. And yet we're talking about God emptying Himself of everything divine, so that He could become everything human—except sin.[148]

And so, for a lifetime—a single human lifetime, or less, since this particular Life was cut off in its prime—God stopped being God (as we conceive of God) and became a Man. For a fleeting moment—an instant in the infinite expanse of eternity—the divine Word—God—became flesh and dwelled among us—as one of us.

The God Who could do anything with His infinite power, could not do this one thing—achieve the salvation—the redemption—of a fallen humanity formed by Him in His image and de-formed by sin—even with all the power He possessed. This defeat of sin in mankind could only be accomplished through weakness. The Deliverer of sinful humanity could only defeat sin by dying at the hand of sin—and dying for sin—the sin in others—and dying as sin—though He never committed a sin.[149] Someone had to die for sin, and yet not deserve to die for sin. In other words, God had to die for sin—no one else could.

And yet, how can the God Who is the Source and Sustainer of all life die? And how can the God Who is perfect holiness—perfect purity—become sin? And how can anyone ever be saved from sin if God cannot—or does not—do the saving?

And so, though it was impossible, God did what had to be done. And to do this impossible thing, God emptied Himself of all the power and wisdom and knowledge and authority and status and splendor that were His, by right and by might. He gave them up.

---

[147] Colossians 1:15-20, ESV.
[148] 2 Corinthians 5:21.
[149] 2 Corinthians 5:21.

There is a line in a popular praise song that says,
> "He gave His life;
> what more could He give?"[150]

And the true answer is, "Quite a lot more." Infinitely more, according to Paul. Jesus Christ gave up His human life. But in becoming Jesus Christ, God could—and did—give up His omnipotence, His omniscience, His omnipresence. He gave up everything about Himself that was divine except the bare and unalterable fact that He *was* divine.

"Oh, how He loved you and me?" If you think all your Savior did was suffer and die for you, you don't know the half of it!

When young David went to fight Goliath to save God's people, Saul, his king, tried to deck David out in his own royal armor. But the shepherd boy took it all off and set it aside, taking only a slingshot and a few river rocks to do battle with the giant.[151]

And when God came to fight the decisive battle with the greater giant, sin, He took off and set aside, not merely the elements of royal armor, but the entirety of His divine defenses, to be born as a helpless Son of David and go into His greatest battle with not even a slingshot or a stone in hand.

The old folks used to sing in the hymn "Rock of Ages,"
> "Nothing in my hand I bring,
> simply to Thy Cross I cling."[152]

And so brought the God Who emptied Himself of His every defense for us: nothing in His hands but the nails that pierced them and pinned Him on His cross.

On that cross, dying as the only Sacrifice that would work to pay for our sins and free us from sin's condemnation, God in Christ had to be God-less—He had to be "man-without-God"—or it wouldn't work; it wouldn't be real. And so, upon the Cross, dying as the Man Who had successfully emptied Himself of His

---

[150] Kurt Kaiser, "Oh, How He Loves You and Me," 1975.
[151] 1 Samuel 17:1-51.
[152] Augustus Montague Toplady, "Rock of Ages," 1763.

rightful divinity, our Christ, our Messiah, our Savior, would cry out in His human agony what so many men and women before Him had cried,

> *"My God, my God, why have you forsaken me?*
> *Why are you so far from saving me...?"*[153]

And the answer was that the God Who had become Man was too close to saving the world for that great victory to be aborted by God saving Himself instead. Christ had chosen to do God's will when it could not be done by God *as God*. And in His dying, as a Man alone, unaided by God, Jesus Christ accomplished God's great purpose in emptying Himself to become man.

Paul said, *"Christ Jesus...emptied himself, by taking the form of a servant, being born in the likeness of men. And being found in human form, he humbled himself by becoming obedient to the point of death, even death on a cross."*

❦

But once He had died—really died—like all humans do and God cannot—*then*, all the infinite, divine power of God could be brought to bear again—for things like raising Jesus from the dead and restoring Him to His rightful place in the Godhead—and restoring to Him all that was rightly His that He had set aside to become our Savior.

God accomplished what He did in Jesus—*as* Jesus—because He emptied Himself *of* Himself. He saw the solution to sin in sacrifice of Self. He took the form of a servant. Though Lord of lords and King of kings, *"He humbled Himself and became obedient."*

And Paul tells the Church, *"Have this mind among yourselves that is yours in Christ Jesus...."*

And the writer of Hebrews says, *"...let us also lay aside every weight... looking to Jesus, the founder and perfecter of our faith, who... endured the cross...and is seated at the right hand of the throne of God."*[154]

---

[153] Psalm 22:1, ESV.
[154] Hebrews 12:1-2, ESV.

Good Friday

So many people in this world are like floundering swimmers, adrift and drowning in an endless sea of sin? Are you one of them?

You cannot save yourself by "taking control" of the situation. The situation is hopeless. Your life is lost if someone doesn't come and help.

And there is help. There is a Lifeguard swimming out to you, but He says, "Let go and let Me save you. Stop grasping to hold onto *Me*—and let *Me* hold onto *you*. If you will let go, nothing will pry you out of My hands."[155]

The Lifesaving God says, "I emptied Myself of everything to save you. Empty yourself of everything to live the life I saved you for. Empty yourself so that I may fill you with the glory and power and wisdom and love I filled Jesus with after He emptied Himself of all the divine attributes that were rightly and eternally His.

God says, *"My strength is made perfect in [your] weakness."*[156] His strength *is* made perfect in your weakness—as it was in the weakness of His Son, Jesus. God says, "Empty yourself of everything you have grasped in this world trying to keep yourself afloat, so that I may fill you with everything I created you to have to live abundantly and forever with the One Who emptied Himself *of* all—and is now exalted *above* all."

"Have this mind in you that was in Christ Jesus."

---

[155] John 10:28-29.
[156] 2 Corinthians 12:9, KJV.

Easter Sunday

The Believe It or Not Story

John 20:1-18 RSV

¹ Now on the first day of the week Mary Mag'dalene came to the tomb early, while it was still dark, and saw that the stone had been taken away from the tomb. ² So she ran, and went to Simon Peter and the other disciple, the one whom Jesus loved, and said to them, "They have taken the Lord out of the tomb, and we do not know where they have laid him." ³ Peter then came out with the other disciple, and they went toward the tomb. ⁴ They both ran, but the other disciple outran Peter and reached the tomb first; ⁵ and stooping to look in, he saw the linen cloths lying there, but he did not go in. ⁶ Then Simon Peter came, following him, and went into the tomb; he saw the linen cloths lying, ⁷ and the napkin, which had been on his head, not lying with the linen cloths but rolled up in a place by itself. ⁸ Then the other disciple, who reached the tomb first, also went in, and he saw and believed; ⁹ for as yet they did not know the scripture, that he must rise from the dead. ¹⁰ Then the disciples went back to their homes.

¹¹ But Mary stood weeping outside the tomb, and as she wept she stooped to look into the tomb; ¹² and she saw two angels in white, sitting where the body of Jesus had lain, one at the head and one at the feet. ¹³ They said to her, "Woman, why are you weeping?" She said to them, "Because they have taken away my Lord, and I do not know where they have laid him." ¹⁴ Saying this, she turned round and saw Jesus standing, but she did not know that it was Jesus. ¹⁵ Jesus said to her, "Woman, why are you weeping? Whom do you seek?" Supposing him to be the gardener, she said to him, "Sir, if you have carried him away, tell me where you have laid him, and I will take him away." ¹⁶ Jesus said to her, "Mary." She turned and said to him in Hebrew, "Rabbo'ni!" (which means Teacher). ¹⁷ Jesus said to her, "Do not hold me, for I have not yet ascended to the Father; but go to my brethren and say to them, I am ascending to my Father and your Father, to my God and your God." ¹⁸ Mary Mag'dalene went and said to the disciples, "I have seen the Lord"; and she told them that he had said these things to her.

19.

The Believe It or Not Story

John 20:1-18 RSV

Well, the nice thing, I suppose, about coming to a worship service on Easter, as opposed to the first Sunday in February or the last Sunday in June, is that you pretty well know what you're going to hear about. Yes, today you will hear the Easter story.

The Bible, from which all sermons should come and some still do, is full of stories, many of which make for great sermons. But these many Bible stories are really all part of one great, big story. It is a great story and it is a big story, and of all the Bible stories that make up this one story, the Easter story is the biggest and greatest part of all.

The Easter story is the heart of everything else. It is an amazing story. It is a "Ripley's Believe It or Not"[157] kind of story. You hear it, and you believe it or you don't. It's a story about life and death, or more accurately, about death and life. The main character in the story is one Jesus of Nazareth. And there are other characters: a woman named Mary, a man named Peter and another man, unnamed—and ultimately, every man, woman and child on earth.

---

[157] A multi-media presentation of odd and unlikely objects, events, persons, and "realities," begun by Robert Ripley in 1918.

The Believe It or Not Story

It reads like science fiction, but it isn't presented as fiction at all. Those who first told the story were the characters *in* the story, and they said it really happened, just the way they told it.

☙❧

But let's face it: this story calls for us to believe the unbelievable. In this world, people who are dead and buried do not come back to life. So if you're having trouble getting your rational mind around the concept of the Resurrection, that's okay; the first disciples of Jesus had the same trouble.

Oh, Mary Magdalene believed in what Jesus had said about God's kingdom. So did Simon Peter, and the other disciple, and all the rest. They just didn't believe that God would put Jesus in charge of the whole thing in the way He did. They believed that the amazing things Jesus did, He did by the power of God, but they did not believe that God would raise Jesus from the dead.

And so, when Jesus was killed, they responded according to what they did believe: they went into grief and shock—and into hiding from the people who might just as easily kill them, too.

And then, contrary to everything in this world, they saw Jesus *alive*. They had not understood that God was *not* going to play by the world's rules. (God doesn't have to, you know.) Jesus did not have to avoid death to live.

Dead?

Yes, certainly—then *alive*!

Bound and beaten and bloody, hanging helpless on a cross, lying lifeless in a grave. Dead.

And now?

Alive!

Death could not hold Him—and don't think it didn't try. But God just pried Jesus out of death's cold, tight grip, and blew the breath of life back into this New Adam in the Garden Tomb, just as He had breathed life into the first Adam in the Garden of

Eden.[158] Jesus came up out of the grave by the power of God—and He *ain't never* going back *again*!

There was no power on earth—or elsewhere—that could stop God from raising Jesus from the dead. And if God can raise Jesus from the dead, He can probably do anything else you can imagine, as well as things beyond your wildest (or holiest) imagination.

"But, in this world, people who are dead and buried do not come back to life."

So maybe we are no longer living in "this world." Maybe, since Jesus was raised from the dead, we are living in "the next world," where God has promised to raise all those who believe in Jesus and accept His atoning sacrifice for their sins. Maybe this is now the world where God has promised to raise them—you—just like He raised Jesus.

How does the song go?
> "And He will raise you up on eagle's wings,
> bear you on the breath of dawn,
> make you to shine like the sun,
> and hold you in the palm of His hand."[159]

Of course, God could have raised Jesus without our ever knowing about it. All He had to do was leave the stone in place—leave everything on the outside of the tomb exactly the way it was—and we would never know.

But God didn't merely want to make Jesus alive again—alive again and forever. God wanted you and me to *know* that Jesus is alive—that God raised Him, not just to live again, but to have eternal life with the power and authority to grant eternal life to us as well.

Jesus did not merely talk about God forgiving and redeeming and reconciling. Jesus was and is the forgiveness of God and the redemption of God and the reconciliation of God—in Person. It was *Him*! It *is* Him! The power of the Resurrection is not in the

---

[158] Genesis 2:5.
[159] Michael Joncas, "On Eagle's Wings," 1976.

story of the Resurrection; it is in the *Person* of the Resurrection to Whom the story of the Resurrection points. The point of the story is to set you looking for Jesus Who is very much alive and can make you very much alive as well. Paul said, *"...in Christ shall all be made alive."*[160]

Now, I cannot prove this to you and I will not try. But neither can those who do *not* want to believe it—and do not want *you* to believe it—prove the Resurrection of Jesus *didn't* happen, no matter how confidently they assure you they have done just that. Nothing can disprove the Resurrection if Jesus is alive.

On the other hand, the Bible story doesn't *prove* the Resurrection, either. It doesn't even explain it. It doesn't really describe it. It just announces it: "There He is, folks: Jesus Christ, dead, buried, *resurrected!* Deal with it."

That's the point of the Easter story. Can I convince you? No. But I can and will invite you and encourage you to let *God* convince you of the reality of the Resurrection and the presence of the living Jesus Christ.

It is not an easy thing to believe in the Resurrection of Jesus— especially today. But if you want to believe, you can. You really can. Just go ahead and believe. Nobody can stop you. You don't even have to know for sure. You just have to want the Resurrection to be so enough that you are willing to give it the benefit of the doubt.

After all, you can't "believe" Jesus into being alive again if He's not, no matter how hard you try. But if Jesus *is* alive, your believing in Him—no matter how tentatively—will "believe" *you* into being alive again, through Him, for all eternity.

༒

Do you believe in the Resurrection? I hope so. Today, the impact of the Resurrection is limited to those who are willing to

---

[160] 1 Corinthians 15:22, RSV.

believe. When Jesus returns at the Last Day, *everyone* will believe in the Resurrection, the willing and the unwilling alike.

Resurrection was certainly not what anybody, friend or foe, expected that Sunday morning. And many today don't expect it, either, no matter how often the story is told. Jesus comes as a real surprise to people who assume He's dead. The last thing they expect is for Jesus to live—really live.

What do you think it would be like to really live? I'm not talking about going wild and throwing decency and restraint to the wind. I'm talking about being so content and confident in your relationship with a living, Resurrected Jesus that you don't need to throw decency or restraint anywhere to feel the joy and excitement of being totally and genuinely alive for a change.

Wow! Living!

So why don't you take a look into this Resurrection business? Even before she knew what the story meant, Mary ran to get somebody to come and look. The stone has been rolled away, but the stone wasn't rolled back to let Jesus *out* of the tomb. The stone was moved to let others *in*, including you. So have a look this morning. If you believe it, you will be different.

You see, if Jesus is alive, the story isn't over. You have to finish the Easter story for yourself—in your life. Jesus went to His grave—and we will go to ours. But Jesus didn't stay in His and neither will we. Where are you going when you finish with your grave—as you will one day? Where are you going when Jesus says to you as He did to Lazarus: *"Come out!"*?[161]

If you drive west across Virginia,[162] you will come to the Blue Ridge Mountains. The road rises up and the view is breathtaking. At some point, you will see a sign that says you have reached "The

---

[161] John 11:43.
[162] This sermon was preached at the chapel of what was then Naval Amphibious Base, Little Creek, in Hampton Roads, Virginia.

Continental Divide." What it means is that, from that point on, everything flows in a different direction.

The Resurrection of Jesus is humanity's "Continental Divide." On Easter morning, in that borrowed tomb, history reached the point where something happened that changed everything. Ultimate reality now flows in a different direction. God raised Jesus from the dead. Now Jesus lives. And when the living Jesus lives in you, something happens that changes everything in you.

Jesus is alive today. How about you?

20.

Easter Come and Easter Go

JOHN 20:1-18 RSV (p. 146)

Do you see the similarities? Like Mary Magdalene, we have come out early—on the first day of the week—to find Someone. Like Mary, we have come to a quiet, garden-like place—though there are no caves or graves on the lovely grounds where we have come today.[163] Nonetheless, Mary's experience may be instructive for us as we seek to find that same Someone Mary sought—and found—early on that day—the first day of the week.

Everyone, including Mary Magdalene, assumed the Someone she was looking for, Jesus of Nazareth, was dead. Many people still do.

Mary came out on Easter morning, expecting to find the dead remnant of her human hope for a better and blessed life. She came to mourn the loss of a unique Person, and the glorious future He proclaimed—and only He could provide.

But she could not find that dead Man. The tomb where they had buried Him was empty.

If you come to Easter looking for a fine historical figure and his noble but frustrated cause, *you* will be frustrated. You will end

---

[163] This sermon was preached at the annual Easter sunrise service held on the grounds of the Pinehurst Resort Hotel in Pinehurst, North Carolina.

up as empty as the tomb Mary found. Easter is not about making peace with death and defeat and disappointment.

Easter is not about grappling with frustration or confusion, either. Mary stood outside an empty tomb, weeping because she could not explain what she had not expected—because she had not imagined God would do what Jesus said His Heavenly Father would do.

When Mary saw an insurmountable obstacle overcome—the massive stone rolled away—she still just wanted to find His body. When she encountered two otherworldly individuals, she never suspected that she might have come to the site of a miracle. When she saw the Jesus she was looking for—alive instead of dead—she did not recognize Him. That's why she asked Him—the One Who now had all the answers to all the questions of time and eternity—that's why she asked Him if He could give her directions to a grave holding "remains" that did not—and never will—exist.

If you come to Easter expecting to make sense of it all within the realm of human thought and understanding, you may be shown empty tombs and supernatural sights and the Savior Himself, but you will not see the reality of His Resurrection that only the eyes of faith can see.

A crucified corpse will always be easier for us to control than a Risen Christ—if we can get our hands on it. But the trouble is, there isn't a corpse like that to be found. And while you're looking, you may look right at the living Lord and take Him for someone else.

In Mary's case, Jesus spoke her name, and she heard His voice, and finally saw Him for Who He was. When *she* was speaking—when *she* was trying to control the situation—she could not see that Jesus, resurrected and triumphant, was right there with her, all the time.

But Jesus called her out of her preoccupation, her concerns, her frantic effort to find the solution to a situation too mysterious for her to manage. And that's when she finally saw, not the One she was looking for, but the One she needed to find.

If you come to Easter thinking you will be able to find Jesus, you will search in vain.

If you come, humbled and willing for Him to speak your name and reveal Himself to you as your Savior and Lord, you will hear and see and know the One Who was crucified, dead and buried—and raised from the dead to rule all of Creation for all of eternity. You will hear Him and see Him and know Him, present with you, right here and right now.

༄༅

Mary Magdalene came out early on the first day of the week to find the mortal remains of Jesus. By the grace of God, she found Jesus in all His immortal glory. But finding more than she came for is not the end of the story, happy though it be.

Easter is not merely the experience of finding Jesus, raised from the dead. We come to Easter to see Jesus, but the Easter Lord is not satisfied just to have us see Him.

We come to Easter—and we are to go from Easter—from our encounter with Jesus—as He directs. "Do not hold Me," He tells Mary, "I am not yours to possess, even now that you see that I am risen from the dead and alive, with you and for you, forever. Do not try to hold Me. Go and tell."

And Mary did as He directed her. She went and said to the disciples (and, no doubt, to many others in the days after Easter), *"I have seen the Lord."* And she told them what Jesus had said to her.

If you have had an Easter experience—if you have heard the Risen Lord speak your name and you have recognized His miraculous, powerful presence in your life—you do not fulfill His purpose in revealing His Resurrection to you if you remain in the "garden" of your encounter with Him. The Easter encounter is not complete without your going and telling what you have heard and seen in His presence. That's what Mary did.

Don't let the similarities end here. You have seen the Lord. He is Risen. Go. Tell.

21.

Have They Taken Away Your Lord?

John 20:1-18 RSV (p. 146)

Today, we gather early on the first day of the week, while it is still dark (or mostly so),[164] to celebrate the Resurrection and sing God's praises. We proclaim, "The Lord is Risen!" We sing, "Alleluia!"

And we are not alone. Around the world, millions and millions are gathered as we are, in gardens green and churches both grand and basic, full of joy and alive with faith, because Jesus is alive—and we know it.

How different it was on that first Easter. It was the first day of the week, but there were no crowds gathered. There was no celebration. Early on that first day of the week, it was still dark. And we need not assume the darkness was limited to the lack of *physical* light.

The very lives of the followers of Jesus had been thrown into darkness by His Crucifixion. The Light of the world had left them.

And the world, without knowing it, was plunged into deep shadow as well, as human sin eclipsed divine radiance, and Jesus died on the Cross.

---

[164] Another outdoor Easter Sunrise Service sermon.

The disciples did not gather together on the morning of that first day of the week. They secluded themselves instead, in grief—and fear. One lone figure—a woman—ventured out into the darkness. She made her way to a garden, but not to worship. She made her way, heavy-hearted, to a tomb, not to proclaim her Christ, but to prepare His corpse for its final and permanent repose.

She went out into a darkness both physical and spiritual, and when she arrived at her destination, the darkness only deepened. Not only had Jesus suffered and died, now His Body was not there. There had been no thought of celebration. Now there would be no consolation, either. Dawn is breaking, and yet darkness reigns.

She rushes off to the disciples who share her sorrow, and proclaims even more sorrow to them: *"They have taken the Lord out of the tomb, and we don't know where they have laid him."*

They have lost their Messiah. Are they now to lose even the memorial of His tomb? They run to the tomb even as she had run from it. They see what she saw, but then they go closer and see more. They see more with their eyes—and more with their souls.

One disciple sees enough to believe—whatever that means. And we do not really know what it does mean because, apparently, even he—even there at the empty tomb—does not yet understand that Jesus must rise from the dead.

They come to the garden. They look in the tomb. They see that the Body of Jesus is not there. But they do not celebrate or sing praises. They go home.

Only the woman remains. And because she does, she will see more than the disciples do. She will see the empty tomb—and she will see angels. She will see a lot, but she still won't "see."

"They have taken away my Lord, and I don't know where...?" she tells the angels she unknowingly encounters. She has come to the tomb, but she doesn't see Jesus.

She doesn't see Jesus. But she's about to.

Jesus is not in the tomb, but "they" haven't taken Him away. "They" haven't taken Him anywhere. He would have to be dead for "them" (or anyone else) to take His Body out of the tomb and put it somewhere else. And dead is the last thing Jesus is—or ever will be again.

Can you see the irony? The woman doesn't know where Jesus is, and He's right there in front of her. She's looking for Jesus at the same time she's looking *at* Jesus and not recognizing Him.

"Woman," He says, standing outside His own tomb.

"Sir," she replies, seeing Him, and yet not seeing that it is *Him*. And then everything changes.

༺༻

"Mary," He says, speaking her name, and in so doing, calling her out of the darkness of death and despair, and into the light of His resurrection.

"Mary!"

"Teacher!"

And what, an hour earlier, no one in the world imagined—what moments before, only one man in all the world *may* have suspected—now, with the call of her name, this woman *sees*—and knows with a certainty that can never be assailed: They have not taken away the Lord—her Lord. He is Risen!

༺༻

There are those today who are desperately trying to take away our Lord. They are trying to take Him away from our classrooms, our courts, our calendars and our currency—away from the places we go and the conversation we share. They would take Him away from our marriages and our children, from our very minds and hearts.

Jesus has always had enemies. They killed Him then, and they're doing their best to kill Him now. The only problem with this on-going compulsion to do Jesus in is that Jesus just keeps on living—keeps on surviving and thriving—coming back to life—coming back to His disciples—despite His enemies' best efforts to be done with Him, once and for all.

For our part, we give the enemies of our Lord too much credit. They haven't taken Him away. They can't. He would have to be dead for that to happen. And dead He is not!

If they could not keep Him in His tomb, they will not be able to keep Him away from us or from anywhere He chooses to be. The best (or worst) they can do is to try to convince you they have. But that's called sleight-of-hand—smoke and mirrors—misdirection—deception—illusion—salesmanship—magic tricks. Don't let them trick you.

Look at the evidence; it's all around you.

The woman looked at the evidence—empty tomb, angels, Jesus risen from the dead—but she drew the wrong conclusion: *"They have taken away my Lord, and I do not know where they have laid him."*

Are you looking at the evidence, and yet still not seeing what it means? Do you not see the truth right before your eyes? Are you bothered—confused—by empty tombs and the self-satisfied assurances of the dedicated cynics and committed disbelievers of our day that they have succeeded in taking Jesus away?

Don't be. Every time you call Jesus your Lord, He's right there, speaking your name? You really don't have to find Him; He comes to you, and waits patiently until you recognize Him.

Have a look. There's light enough to see. It's early, but the darkness is gone. The Light of the world has risen.

22.

Today's the Day!

John 20:1-18 RSV (p. 146)

Today is my birthday.

This year, my birthday falls on Easter. The last time Easter fell on April 5th was 62 years ago—the day I was born. I have been waiting for this day, April 5th, 2015, my whole life—or at least since I was old enough to know that I was born on Easter Sunday, and capable enough to find out when my birthday and Easter would once again coincide. It has taken a very long time for this convergence to take place, but today's the day!

And yet, it doesn't matter at all. This convergence is, in truth, merely a curious coincidence of no significance, even for me. Nothing will happen to me or to anyone else, now or later, because my mother happened to give birth to me on Easter Sunday, or because I celebrate the day of my entry into this world on Easter for the first time in my life this year.

Having your birthday fall on a holiday is an "intersection" empty of any real importance. People born on the Fourth of July will not necessarily be free. You can celebrate your birthday on Thanksgiving and not be grateful for anything. Not everyone whose birthday falls on Christmas is a Christian. That today my birthday falls on Easter?

No big deal.

But that today *is* Easter means *everything*! Whatever the day you or I came out of the womb to begin our physical lives on this earth, the day Jesus came out of the tomb to begin His resurrected life—and to begin ours, too, if we believe in His Resurrection—is the most significant date on the calendar *every* year. It is the most significant day in all of human history.

೭⊷ଛ

And *today's* the day!

Easter Sunday—the first one—was a day that many people had been waiting for—and for far longer than 62 years. Generations of God's people had waited for hundreds of years—and far more people than that, who did not even know God cared for them, or what they were waiting for, had spent their whole lives knowing they needed something to change to make their lives different—better—right—in a way they did not understand, but felt, nonetheless.

And then one day, what all the world had been waiting for—happened. The One Who could change the world and everybody in it—did. On this day, a mysterious and magnetic Man, in an odd and out of the way place, proclaiming radical but reassuring ideas about one particular God—a Man Who had been put to death in a profoundly permanent way for His trouble—wasn't dead any more.

And He wasn't just "not dead." He was alive in a way that no one had ever been alive before, whatever the day on which they were born. He was alive in a way that every man, woman and child before and since that day *want* to be alive, whether they admit it to themselves or not. And that miraculous Man went from dead to alive early on the Sunday morning we now call Easter.

And *today's* the day.

೭⊷ଛ

Easter Sunday

But even though today is Easter—the "birthday," if you will, of the Risen Lord—most people have seen no benefit—no change—in their lives, whatever their birthdays. Easter—even as the most important day in history—will not by itself bring about the new life that can only come about because of what happened on Easter. Easter—the date of the Resurrection of Jesus—must coincide, it turns out, with your birthday after all.

Just not your biological birthday. You have to have Easter. And you have to have *your* "re-birth" day. Just as Jesus was dead and then miraculously, gloriously, eternally alive by the power of God, so you and I and every person who draws breath must one day give birth to the seed of faith God has implanted in our souls. The "birthday" of Christ reborn must come together with the birthday of our faith—or, wonderful as Easter is, it won't "work."

Am I confusing you? Well, you won't be the first to be confused. Jesus Himself did a pretty good job of leaving a pretty good Bible scholar at a loss when He told a man named Nicodemus: *"…unless one is born again he cannot see the kingdom of God."*[165]

You can almost hear the man sputtering in response: *"How can a man be born when he is old? Can he enter a second time into his mother's womb and be born?"*[166]

And Jesus said, "Nope. That's not the kind of birthday I'm talking about. You've got to have a birth of faith."

For a few people, their spiritual birthday actually did coincide with Easter, the first time around. At least one of the two disciples who ran to the empty tomb, and saw what was there, "believed," according to John. And then Mary Magdalene met Jesus a little later on His Rise-from-the-Dead-to-Eternal-Life Day, and her faith in His Resurrection was born as well. Later still, there would be multiple births of faith when the Risen Christ passed through

---

[165] John 3:3, ESV.
[166] John 3:4, ESV.

locked doors and appeared to His disciples in a room they thought no one could enter—especially Him.[167]

And when faith in the Resurrection is born in any human heart, the person in whom that faith is born hears the call God spoke through Isaiah the prophet proclaiming the coming salvation of God,

> *"Arise, shine, for your light has come,*
> *and the glory of the Lord has risen upon you.*
> *…the Lord will arise upon you,*
> *…the Lord will be your everlasting light…."*[168]

※

What's Isaiah talking about?

A spiritual birthday party: The Lord of Easter Resurrection coming into your life to celebrate with you *your* birth of faith in the Resurrection and in the living Lord of the Resurrection.

Do you remember the date of your "spiritual birthday"—the day your faith in Jesus was born?

Most of us don't, really, and some of us would say that it's hard to pinpoint a particular day because our faith grew gradually in the nurturing womb of our home or our church or some other spiritual support group until it was viable in the world around us.

But if your faith in Jesus is alive, as He is alive, then at some point in your life, faith was born. And Easter is the perfect day to celebrate it—to celebrate together with Jesus Who came back—was "born" back—to life on this day.

And you are not alone. What the writer of Hebrews wrote about Abraham seems just as true of Jesus: *"…from one man, and him as good as dead, were born…as many as the stars of heaven…."*[169]

---

[167] John 20:19-29.
[168] Isaiah 60:1-2, ESV.
[169] Hebrews 11:12, ESV.

John said, *"...to all who... believed in his name, he gave the right to become children of God, who were born, not of blood nor of the will of the flesh nor of the will of man, but of God."*[170] The birth of faith.

The First Epistle of John says, *"Everyone who believes that Jesus is the Christ has been born of God...."*[171]

Do you get the gist of things here? *"As many as...,"* *"....to all who believe...,"* *"everybody who believes..."* We are talking one whopping, wonderful combination Easter/faith-birthday party.

And Peter writes, *"...you have been born again, not of perishable seed but of imperishable, through the living and abiding word of God...,"*[172] which means that, in addition to the Risen Lord coming to your birthday party of faith, He comes bringing great birthday gifts: Resurrection joy, Resurrection power, Resurrection peace, Resurrection life.

❧

It has been 62 years since my biological birthday last fell on Easter. The two events will come together again in 11 years, I've discovered, and again, 11 years after that, and 11 years after that. I confess, I'm a little curious as to which of those birthdays I'll still be around for.

But it really doesn't matter. I'll have a birthday every year I'm here, on whatever day it falls. And when I'm no longer here, I'll stop celebrating *that* birthday forever.

But I will never stop celebrating Easter, the day God gave new life to His only-begotten Son Who was *born in the likeness of men,*[173] and then was born from death to eternal life. That's why I'm celebrating today.

And I'll never stop celebrating the birthday of my faith in Him, because, together, those two days ensure that I will always be alive

---

[170] John 1:12-13, ESV.
[171] 1 John 5:1, ESV.
[172] 1 Peter 1:23, ESV.
[173] Philippians 2:7, ESV.

to celebrate them—*like* Jesus, and *with* Jesus—for all eternity, whether here or in heaven.

In fact, if I interpret scripture correctly, you and I and everybody in heaven will be celebrating those two days every day in heaven, because, as Isaiah says,

"The sun shall be no more your light by day…
for the Lord will be your everlasting light,"[174]

…which means the sun will not mark the days for us any more by its rising and setting. The Lord, our everlasting Light, will create for us everlasting day.

ം൭

One of the most important things they had to figure out in the early years of the Church was what day was the right day to celebrate Easter each year. As you may have noticed, it's a holiday that "floats" from day to day, year by year. It's a complicated calculation; you may not want to attempt it at home.

But you can celebrate the Resurrection of our Savior, and the birth of your faith in Him, every day, because the power of the Resurrection and the reality of your faith in Jesus, alive and eternal, come together every day to ensure your salvation and your life with Him, today and tomorrow and always. When your faith is alive and Jesus is alive, "today" is *always* "the day."

Let me give the Apostle Peter the last word:

"Blessed be the God and Father of our Lord Jesus Christ! According to his great mercy, he has caused us to be born again to a living hope through the resurrection of Jesus Christ from the dead…."[175]

Happy "Re-birth" Day!

He is Risen!

ം൭

---

[174] Isaiah 60:19-20, ESV.
[175] 1 Peter 1:3, ESV.

23.

You Can Kill Him, But…

John 20:1-18 RSV (p. 146)

Mary Magdalene went looking for a dead man. Early on that Sunday morning, before the sun came up or anybody else had crawled out of bed, Mary was on a mission to find the Body of her beloved Healer,[176] Teacher, and hoped-for Messiah, Jesus. She knew the Body was there. She had seen where they laid Him. She knew He was dead—she had watched, helpless, while they killed Him.

Powerful men had conspired to kill this Jesus of Nazareth[177] and they had done their lethal work well. They had maneuvered an indifferent official to order brutal executioners to take away His life—methodically, callously and completely.[178] And when the gruesome deed was done —when, as Jesus Himself said, *"It is finished,"*[179] they ripped His bloody corpse down off the cross and turned it over to others, who hustled it into a borrowed grave and hurried away, racing the setting sun to their destinations for the night.

---

[176] Luke 8:2.
[177] John 11:45-53.
[178] John 19.
[179] John 19:30, NRSV.

They left Him, dead, to the darkness. And later, also in the darkness, Mary came looking for Jesus where—and how—they had left Him.

❧

But the Body wasn't there. The Body of Jesus wasn't to be found—there or anywhere. His Body—His dead corpse—wouldn't be found anywhere ever again.

Those who had taken His life so cheerfully and confidently on that Friday were apparently ignorant of one of the fundamental facts of the universe: you can kill Him, but He won't stay dead. You can kill Jesus, but He will shortly rise again.

This fundamental fact was demonstrated to Mary Magdalene when she went out in the dark, early on that first day of the week, to find this dead Man she had seen them kill. What she found was a stone out of place, a tomb without a body—and, finally, a Jesus Who was very much alive.

To say she was astounded—amazed—would be an understatement. Not that Jesus hadn't told her—and others—that He would be killed and then rise from the dead.[180]

But whips and spears, spikes and crosses speak with an impressive authority about the seeming finality of death. They make it hard to believe the life-after-death assurances of One Who will give His life without reservation into the hands of those who will take His life without reluctance or remorse.

They killed Jesus—and yet there He was—standing before her, speaking her name, giving her a mission. They killed Jesus, just as they intended. But there He was—alive—*hardly* as they intended. And though He didn't waste any time appearing to those who had killed Him, it wouldn't be long before they, too, discovered that He was alive—and that there was nothing they could do about it.

---

[180] Mark 8:31; Luke 9:22.

Easter Sunday

Not that they didn't try, of course. They did everything they could think of to kill Him again, which would be difficult given that He ascended to heaven and sits at the right hand of the Father in glory, somewhat beyond their reach.[181]

☙❧

So they settled for trying to kill the awareness of people that Jesus is alive—and the faith of people in His promise of redemption and salvation. They tried to kill the experience of the abiding presence and power of Jesus, and the submission of His followers to His spiritual and moral authority.

The enemies of Jesus tried to kill Him wherever and however they could. And every time they thought they had succeeded—every time they started passing out the cigars and "high-fiving" each other for doing away with Jesus—it wasn't long before He appeared to someone and showed that He was very much alive.

You would think they would learn, over the years, these self-assigned enemies of Jesus. You would think they would eventually realize that when you think you've killed Jesus, He just keeps rising again. But they apparently don't, because they're still trying to kill Him, even today.

In some parts of our world, their methods are chillingly similar to those used on Jesus Himself. If Jesus lives in the heart and mind of someone—kill that someone, suddenly and viciously. If Jesus lives in many people—kill them all. Single them out as servants of the living Christ and attack them with an animal savagery.

In some parts of our world, whole families, whole churches, whole communities are brutally killed, just to kill the Jesus Who is in them. But Jesus rises up and is reborn in the hearts of others who walk in the footsteps of the martyrs and know from personal experience that He is Risen.

---

[181] Mark 16:19.

And here in our own country, where Pilgrims prayed and freedom rings, the enemies of Jesus are still determined to do Him in. Their schemes are more sophisticated; their weapons more intellectual and economic than physical. But their goal is the same and their results are, by all outward appearances, very effective.

Some of His enemies are determined to kill Jesus with the superiority of empirical science. They delight in pointing out how this scientific discovery or that—this or that well-known theory of chemistry or physics, astronomy or geology, anatomy or medicine—widely accepted throughout the scientific community—undermines the central claims of Christianity about the person of Jesus.

Their "killer" argument is that what Christians believe about Jesus is not scientifically possible—the scientific evidence will not support it, and may, in fact, disprove it. According to "Science," everybody dies, one way or another, and dead people—people who are truly dead as the Bible assures us Jesus was—do not come back to life.

The scientific enemies of Jesus kill Him on a cross of empirical evidence. And many who respect science see them do this and mourn the demise of a Jesus Who (they are sure) could not survive the crucifixion of modern scientific scrutiny.

The only problem is that other people, even some scientists, look at the same heavens and the same earth—they look at the same elements of chemistry and laws of physics—they look at the marvel of the human body and the miracles of modern medicine (and the miracles that baffle modern medicine), and they come face to face with the Risen Christ.

His scientific enemies can kill Him, but He just keeps turning up alive. Maybe that's because,

"The earth is the Lord's and the fullness thereof, the world and they that dwell therein."[182]

---

[182] Psalm 24:1, KJV.

Easter Sunday

There are others in our day who are determined to kill Jesus with a superior understanding of the human mind. Armed with the psychological suggestions of Freud and Jung and Adler[183] and others, the enemies of Jesus attack Him as a figment of our collective imaginations. They say Jesus was deluded in life, which, they assure us, ended for good with His fatal session on the Cross.

His followers, then and now, they say, are equally deluded and fixated on a fantasy that allows them to avoid the unpleasant truth of their own mortality. In other words, these enemies would kill Jesus in you by telling you that to believe Jesus is alive is to be a bit insane: so bury Him for the sake of your mental health.

It's another "killer" argument, and many have mentally assigned Jesus to the grave as a result. But the one Person they haven't convinced is Jesus, Who, according to scripture, knew the human mind so well that people had the sense He was reading their thoughts.[184] It was Jesus Who put true lunatics in their right minds.[185]

And when He was raised from the dead, Jesus eased the minds of those who saw Him alive.[186]

"You just think Jesus is alive," His enemies say. Mary just thought He was alive, too—because she saw Him and heard Him. We think Jesus is alive because, as Paul says, Jesus appeared to Peter and the disciples, to hundreds of other followers, to James and the Apostles and to Paul himself.[187]

And Jesus, alive and glorified, appears to us—even as His enemies are convinced they have finally killed Him for good.

---

[183] Sigmund Freud, 1856-1939, was the founder of psychoanalysis. Carl Jung, 1875-1961, was the founder of analytical psychology. Alfred Adler, 1870-1937, was the founder of individual psychology.
[184] Matthew 9:4.
[185] Mark 5:1-15.
[186] John 20:19-22.
[187] 1 Corinthians 15:3-8.

You Can Kill Him, But...

The enemies of Jesus are all over these days, trying so hard to kill Him off. They are in our schools, determined to suffocate Him by locking Him away from any involvement in the lives and learning of our children. And then He rises, alive in the hearts of the boys and girls who see their need for more than the lessons of man, and see in Jesus the answer to the greatest test of all.

The enemies of Jesus are in the entertainment industry, crucifying Him with distortion and distain in feature films and documentaries, in dark lyrics and darker videos. By the power of pretense, the "artists" of our day assure us that Jesus is dead and that no one need care about His will—for our lives or our world. "Follow us, instead," say the famous faces, "Focus on our exploits and adopt our views."

But powerful as they are, the stars of stage and screen and recording studio cannot prevent Jesus from living above and beyond their temporary celebrity and holding them accountable for the shipwreck they make of their own lives and their impact on the unsuspecting masses they lead astray.

❦

So what do you do when you live in a world where so many people are obsessed with nailing Jesus to their favorite contemporary crosses?

You do like Mary Magdalene did and get up early on the first day of the week—and on the second and on the third, and so on—and go to where you know Him to be.

You get up and go looking for Jesus, not on the crosses of contempt or in the tombs of ridicule and irrelevance. You look for Him in your heart and in the world around you, the world of nature and the world of human events as well. You go looking, not for the corpse they're very proud to have created, but for the risen, living and lordly Christ they can never prevent from coming out of whatever grave they try to stuff Him into.

Mary was looking for the Man they had killed and buried. That Man no longer existed. He had become the Resurrected Savior, the Great High Priest, the ascended Son of God, alive for evermore.

And now—even now—for every enemy who is sure that Jesus is dead, there is another person who discovers the Risen Christ, hears His words and sees His face and knows that He is alive. Mary was that person on that first Easter Sunday. Perhaps you are that person today.

Halleluiah! Jesus is not dead. He is Risen! He is alive!

Easter Sunday

Deuteronomy 30:15-20 ESV

[15] *"See, I have set before you today life and good, death and evil.* [16] *If you obey the commandments of the* LORD *your God that I command you today, by loving the* LORD *your God, by walking in his ways, and by keeping his commandments and his statutes and his rules, then you shall live and multiply, and the* LORD *your God will bless you in the land that you are entering to take possession of it.* [17] *But if your heart turns away, and you will not hear, but are drawn away to worship other gods and serve them,* [18] *I declare to you today, that you shall surely perish. You shall not live long in the land that you are going over the Jordan to enter and possess.* [19] *I call heaven and earth to witness against you today, that I have set before you life and death, blessing and curse. Therefore choose life, that you and your offspring may live,* [20] *loving the* LORD *your God, obeying his voice and holding fast to him, for he is your life and length of days, that you may dwell in the land that the* LORD *swore to your fathers, to Abraham, to Isaac, and to Jacob, to give them."*

Life, If You Will Have It

Matthew 28:1-10 ESV

¹ Now after the Sabbath, toward the dawn of the first day of the week, Mary Magdalene and the other Mary went to see the tomb. ² And behold, there was a great earthquake, for an angel of the Lord descended from heaven and came and rolled back the stone and sat on it. ³ His appearance was like lightning, and his clothing white as snow. ⁴ And for fear of him the guards trembled and became like dead men. ⁵ But the angel said to the women, "Do not be afraid, for I know that you seek Jesus who was crucified. ⁶ He is not here, for he has risen, as he said. Come, see the place where he lay. ⁷ Then go quickly and tell his disciples that he has risen from the dead, and behold, he is going before you to Galilee; there you will see him. See, I have told you." ⁸ So they departed quickly from the tomb with fear and great joy, and ran to tell his disciples. ⁹ And behold, Jesus met them and said, "Greetings!" And they came up and took hold of his feet and worshiped him. ¹⁰ Then Jesus said to them, "Do not be afraid; go and tell my brothers to go to Galilee, and there they will see me."

24.

Life, If You Will Have It

Deuteronomy 30:15-20; Matthew 28:1-10 ESV

Today is Easter. Christ is Risen. And you have seen the angel or heard the women or run into Jesus Himself, very much alive, and far more than well. You believe what you have seen or heard or experienced about the Resurrection.

Or you don't. Or you don't know if you do or not because the very idea of anybody dead and buried coming back to life is unbelievable, you're told, by people who ought to know what they're talking about—except that millions *have* believed it, with all their hearts, and millions more still believe it today, including most of us here, which itself is unbelievable to those who don't believe in the Resurrection to start with.

But let's clear up a little confusion about this "believing" business right at the beginning: What you believe about the Resurrection has no impact on the reality of the Resurrection. Your believing in the Resurrection does not make it so. Your *not* believing in the Resurrection does not make it *not* so. The reality of the Resurrection is independent of what anybody believes about it—and what *everybody* believes about it. It *is*, or it *isn't*, regardless of what you believe.

And so you believe or you don't, or don't know if you do or you don't.

But whatever you believe about the Resurrection, you believe it *in faith*. Even *dis*believing is an act of faith—negative faith, of course—but faith, nonetheless. What you believe, you believe in faith because there is no way to prove the truth of what you believe before you believe it, whatever it is that you believe.

You can't prove to me the Resurrection didn't happen, and I can't prove to you—if you do not believe it—that the Resurrection did happen. Each of us has looked at a certain set of clues—a body of evidence—and chosen to believe something about the Resurrection—or perhaps not to believe anything, supposing no position on the matter is better than going one way or the other in the absence of absolute proof.

So, do we just shake hands, and all go our separate ways?

We could—except that lack of "proof" does not mean lack of consequences. What you believe about the Resurrection does not determine whether it happened or not. But the truth about the Resurrection will have tremendous consequences on you and your family and your descendants and your community and your country and the world, based on what you believe about it. In other words, what you believe about the Resurrection matters.

Of course, if the Resurrection did not take place, it won't matter much, whether you believe it did or not. Believers in a Resurrection that didn't happen will have wasted an awful lot of time and treasure, forming congregations and building churches, living morally and serving sacrificially. We will have whatever joy and love we have experienced while we shared our faith in "the Resurrection that didn't happen," but, as the Apostle Paul anticipated even in the New Testament,[188] we will have deserved all the ridicule we received from those who thought our faith was…well…ridiculous.

---

[188] 1 Corinthians 15:13-19.

Easter Sunday

The non-believers will have the satisfaction after they die of knowing they were right all along, if it turns out there was no Resurrection, except that they won't have *any* satisfaction, really, because they won't know anything, because there will be no resurrection of the dead if Christ wasn't raised, so they and everybody else will just be dead.

But the idea of just being dead forever seems to make them pretty happy now. And maybe that will be enough if, as they believe, there's nothing "on the other side."

But if—as the Apostle Paul and all four gospels and all the eyewitnesses and everything in the New Testament and hundreds of millions of Christians since claim—Jesus was raised from the dead, then the business of consequences takes on a whole different flavor. If your faith in the Resurrection turns out to be well-founded, you'll know it. And the consequences for you will be every wonderful thing God promised, and infinitely more, really, because the Bible can only convey the part of salvation that can be conceived in the human mind and expressed in human language, which can't be much when you consider that the God making the promises can raise you from the dead like He did Jesus and reward you with eternal life in heaven—which He created all of, all by Himself, by the way, in addition to the earth.[189]

And if it turns out that God did raise Jesus from the dead, those who didn't believe it will know it, too. "Significant consequences" doesn't begin to describe what will await them. You kind of wish the boundaries of human imagination were the limits of what they have in store.

Oh, and just to clarify: The Bible says that the God Who raised Jesus from the dead only recognizes *two* categories when it comes to belief about the Resurrection.[190] There are those who *do* choose to believe in the Resurrection—and those who *don't* choose to

---

[189] Genesis 1:1.
[190] Matthew 12:30; Romans 10:8-9.

believe in the Resurrection. There is no third category for those who choose to withhold judgment.

Have you picked up on the phrase that keeps recurring: "choose to believe"?

Belief is a choice, whatever you believe. Proof forces acceptance. There is no choice involved when the matter in question is "proven."

'But faith is different. The French scientist Blaise Pascal said four centuries ago, "In faith, there is enough light for those who want to believe and enough shadow to blind those who don't."[191] In faith, you choose. You choose to believe in the Resurrection or not. And you are responsible for the consequences of what you choose to believe in.

ೞ‑ೞ

But all the consequences are not reserved for the "hereafter." When God raised Jesus from the dead, He placed a simple choice about this world before you as well. It wasn't a new choice. God's prophet, Moses, put the choice before God's people a thousand years and more before God put it to the world again in the Resurrection. What did Moses say? *"Today I have set before you, life and death."*

That is the message of the Resurrection. The Resurrection is God setting before you the basic choice of your existence: life or death. The world took the life of Jesus. God restored it—and more.

"Which will it be?" says God, "You can have life or death."

What is life?

According to Moses, it's prosperity—blessings—many years—many joys—the gift of a gracious and loving God to guide and provide.

And death?

---

[191] Blaise Pascal, *Pensees*, 1669.

Easter Sunday

Adversity—heartache and hardship—disappointment and destruction of dreams and hopes—the curse of a life unfolding without God. "I have set before you—and you must choose to believe in—either life or death. You must choose one or the other. You *will* choose one or the other."

To choose life is to choose to believe in the God Who gave life to Jesus at the Resurrection and gives it to all who will believe in Him. To choose death, whether you mean to or not, is both to choose the world that, without God, is devoted to darkness and destruction, and to choose a non-existent neutrality between the life-giving God and the life-taking world.

What you choose to believe about the Resurrection and the God behind it will determine what your life will be like, both in this world and the next. If you believe in the Resurrection, you begin to experience your own resurrected life. The process is not postponed until you are "dead and gone."

When you choose to believe, you also choose to live. All your choices begin pointing in the direction of life. You enter more and more into a way of living that is blessed with the benefits of God's grace. Your belief leads you to make choices that bring you into harmony with the will of God rather than keeping you in opposition to God. And day after day at first, then year after year, you discover your life being lived out ever more clearly in the power and providence of God.

In the same way, a life lived in denial of the Resurrection will, over time, show the cumulative impact of the absence of the God Who gives life its abundance.[192]

☙❧

And there's one more thing. Though the Resurrection cannot be proved according to the criteria of the world, it can be confirmed in the life of the person who believes it in faith. Just as

---
[192] John 10:10.

God told Moses that He would meet the children of Israel at Mount Sinai *after* they trusted God to deliver them from Egypt (the land obsessed with death, by the way),[193] so the Risen Christ sent word for His disciples to meet Him in Galilee. When they chose to believe—when the Hebrews went to Mount Sinai and the disciples to Galilee—they both found that their divine Savior was there, just as He said He would be.

When you choose to believe in the Resurrection—when you choose life—you enter into a life lived in joyful obedience to God and loving covenant with God. And God confirms in your life and experience that the Resurrection and its power are real—that His promise to you of blessed, abundant life is real—because you find the Risen Christ alive in you.

"But you can't prove the Resurrection!"

Not to you, maybe. But I've lived long enough believing in the Resurrection that I have received all the confirmation *I* need. I believe more now than I ever have before. I have watched the lives of others who have chosen to believe in the Resurrection and seen the confirmation in their lives, too. And I have observed the lives of those who have chosen not to believe, and I have seen what happens when you do not choose life.

Because I believe in the Resurrection, I experience the Resurrection—now. My life has been "a foretaste of glory divine"[194]—not because of me being good, but because of God being God—because I choose to believe that God has done what the Bible said He has, and that He will do all the things He said He would.

God raised Jesus from the dead. And because I believe that, God has been raising me from the dead, too—every day—and giving me life. I chose to believe; God chose to confirm my faith in the Resurrection.

---

[193] Exodus 3:12.
[194] Fanny Crosby, "Blessed Assurance," 1873.

Easter Sunday

Today is Easter. Christ is Risen. God is offering you life instead of death. You can have life, here and hereafter. Believe it, and you will have it.

ॐ

His Resurrection—and Yours

Romans 6:3-11 ESV

³ Do you not know that all of us who have been baptized into Christ Jesus were baptized into his death? ⁴ We were buried therefore with him by baptism into death, in order that, just as Christ was raised from the dead by the glory of the Father, we too might walk in newness of life.

⁵ For if we have been united with him in a death like his, we shall certainly be united with him in a resurrection like his. ⁶ We know that our old self was crucified with him in order that the body of sin might be brought to nothing, so that we would no longer be enslaved to sin. ⁷ For one who has died has been set free from sin. ⁸ Now if we have died with Christ, we believe that we will also live with him. ⁹ We know that Christ, being raised from the dead, will never die again; death no longer has dominion over him. ¹⁰ For the death he died he died to sin, once for all, but the life he lives he lives to God. ¹¹ So you also must consider yourselves dead to sin and alive to God in Christ Jesus.

25.

His Resurrection—and Yours

Romans 6:3-11; Matthew 28:1-10 ESV (p. 176)

Easter: The Resurrection Day of Jesus. Crucified on the Cross. Buried in the tomb. Raised from the dead.

Easter: The Resurrection of Jesus—and everything that means. Preachers around the world today will proclaim it. Sunday School teachers will explain it. Apologists will defend it. Believers will rejoice over it as the greatest thing in the world—which it is.

The Resurrection of Jesus is the bedrock core of Christianity. It is the heart of the Gospel of salvation—the main thing we tell the world about Jesus, and the main thing we take to heart about what *we* have been told. On this day, more than any other, we celebrate the Resurrection of Jesus, the miracle to which all the mighty acts of God in history before it moved and pointed.

Because of His Resurrection, we recognize that Jesus is Christ and Lord and God. Because of His Resurrection, we know that, in all Jesus said, God was speaking powerfully and truthfully to us—and in all Jesus did, He intentionally and accurately demonstrated God's divine nature, and God's eternal purpose for His Creation.

His Resurrection—and Yours

Jesus was dead—as dead as you can get. And then, He was *alive*—and *is* alive—and will always *be* alive—forever. His Resurrection guarantees it.

And how wonderful for Jesus! He is alive again—as alive as we are, and yet, infinitely more alive than we are, because His life no longer awaits death as its inevitable conclusion. For Jesus, death no longer colors every consideration with the perspective imposed by the lurking fear of a final day—a final breath—a final flash of consciousness before all is lost in a darkness that never ends.

No, Jesus has been raised from the dead—from that death. And we celebrate for Him.

It couldn't have happened to a nicer guy—or one more deserving. In fact, except for Jesus, it couldn't have happened to anyone deserving at all.

❧

But the greatest thing about the Resurrection of Jesus is not what it means for Jesus. The greatest thing about the Resurrection of Jesus—the reason Easter Sunday is such a glorious day—is what His Resurrection means for *you*.

To put it simply: His Resurrection is the guarantee of *yours*—if you believe in His, and the promise of the One Who raised Him *to raise you, too*. So, on this Easter, this Resurrection Day (of Jesus), let us consider—and celebrate—*your* Easter, *your* resurrection day.

That's what Paul is doing in the portion of his letter to the believers in Rome that we read earlier: *"...we shall certainly be united with Him in a resurrection like his."*

It's not unusual to think about your own death, especially if you've got a lot of life in your rearview mirror, or if your health or your work or your circumstances make it more possible, or even likely, that your death will not be a long way off. But how often and how deeply do you think about your own resurrection?

Let's think about it now.

The Bible is pretty clear that you've got a resurrection coming.

Jesus said, *"For this is the will of my Father, that everyone who looks on the Son and believes in him should have eternal life, and I will raise him up on the last day."*[195]

Paul wrote, *"Jesus died and rose again. Even so—through Jesus—God will bring with him those who have fallen asleep. For the Lord himself will descend from heaven with a cry of command, with the voice of an archangel, and with the sound of the trumpet of God. And the dead in Christ will rise...."*[196]

Paul told the Corinthians, *"God raised the Lord and will also raise us up by his power."*[197]

Here's how it works: If you believe in the Resurrection of Jesus, you've got a resurrection of your own coming.

And what is *your* resurrection going to be like?

Paul says, *"What is sown* (meaning your physical body, which he likens to a seed)—*What is sown is perishable; what is raised is imperishable. It is sown in dishonor; it is raised in glory. It is sown in weakness; it is raised in power. It is sown a natural body; it is raised a spiritual body. ...in a moment, in the twinkling of an eye, at the last trumpet. For the trumpet will sound, and the dead will be raised imperishable, and we shall be changed."*[198]

So, when you are raised from the dead, you will never have to "deal" with death again. You will be im-perish-able.

What's more: when you are raised from the dead, there will be nothing about you that will, in any way, embarrass you, frustrate you, disappoint you, or diminish you. Everything about you will be perfect. You will be completely covered in the glory of God.

When you are raised from the dead, not only will you not have to struggle with all the things you could not do well enough—or at all—in this life—not only will there be no temptations to contend with—you will always and forever be able to do everything you

---

[195] John 6:40, ESV.
[196] 1 Thessalonians 4:14, 16, ESV.
[197] 1 Corinthians 6:14, ESV.
[198] 1 Corinthians 15:42-44, 52, ESV.

His Resurrection—and Yours

need and want to do—and do them absolutely perfectly. And the only things you will want to do are the things you should do.

You will know and remember and understand, just as perfectly, everything you should and want to know and remember and understand.

People accumulate weaknesses over the course of this life. You will be raised by and in God's infinite spiritual power with no weaknesses when you are resurrected.

Your resurrection will be spectacular, far more so than the relatively subdued Resurrection Jesus experienced. When you are raised from the dead, the whole world will know it immediately. Jesus will be there in all His divine majesty to raise you up. Angels will fill the sky. And trumpets will sound from heaven like no sound ever heard on earth.

And when He raises you to life again, you will know, immediately, that you are "you"—and you will know just as certainly that you are more than you ever were before—because when you are raised from the dead, you will be changed. You will be imperishable, glorious, powerful, spiritual.

On Easter Sunday, Christians sing, "Up from the grave He arose!"[199] On *your* resurrection day, you and all those who will be raised with you can sing,

> "Up from the grave we arose!"
> "Low in the grave we lay—
> (like) Jesus my Savior!
> Waiting the coming day—
> (of) Jesus my Lord!"

And then, on that day:

> "Up from the grave we arose,
> With a mighty triumph o'er our foes.
> We arose the victor[s] from the dark domain,
> And we live forever with His saints to reign.

---

[199] George C. Hugg, "He Arose," 1891.

Easter Sunday

>He arose! We arose!
>Hallelujah!
>Christ—and we—arose!

Am I being silly—or sacrilegious? I don't think so.

The Son of God did not give up His exalted place in heaven and come to this earth and endure all that He endured—including and especially His Crucifixion[200]—so that *He* could be raised. He did all that—went through all that—for *your* resurrection. He died so that *you* could be raised. He was raised so that *you* would be, too. Otherwise, how would you know to believe—in His Resurrection—*and* yours?

Do you believe in the Resurrection of Jesus? If so, you've got a resurrection of your own coming. Guaranteed!

༄

But what about now? What about this time between His Resurrection and yours? What about every day you have left in this life that is anything but what you've been promised for the next?

The truth is that His Resurrection has benefits for you even before you experience the resurrection He made possible for you. Before His Crucifixion, Jesus lived His life with an unwavering conviction that the God Who sent Him would preserve Him for eternity—come what may in this life.

And in like manner, with similar conviction, we sing:

>"Because He lives, I can face tomorrow.
>Because He lives, all fear is gone.
>Because I know He holds the future—
>Life is worth the living, just because He lives."[201]

Because Jesus lives, you know that your resurrection is right around the corner—and that *until* you turn that corner—that last corner of *this* life—tomorrow—and every tomorrow after that—

---

[200] Philippians 2:5-8.
[201] Bill Gaither, "Because He Lives," 1999.

will be a day spent in the loving fellowship—and the joyful service—of Jesus Christ, your Risen Savior.

Because He lives, everything you would normally and reasonably be afraid of is redefined as something that He has the power and will to overcome for you—something that you will one day leave behind—something you *can* leave behind because it will not be a part of the eternal life you spend with Him—something that is not a part of the future He holds in trust for you in anticipation of your resurrection.[202]

Because Jesus lives, even *this* life is worth living.

༄༅

But, of course, you're not really living this life any more. You gave it up—crucified it—buried it—with Jesus—so that you could have a resurrected life like His, instead.

What did Paul say?

"We know that our old self was crucified with him... We were buried...with him by baptism into death, in order that, just as Christ was raised from the dead by the glory of the Father, we, too, might walk in newness of life. Now, if we have died with Christ...we will also live with him."

Did Jesus have to wait until He was resurrected to live like He would when He *was* resurrected? Or did His faith in His Heavenly Father enable Him to live that eternal life with its remarkable power, glory and wonder in the midst of the frustration, frailty and fleetingness of this life?

And does *your* faith in the Resurrection of Jesus not enable you—and entitle you—to live your life like He lived His—to live your life in *this* world as "a foretaste of glory divine"[203]?

Because His resurrection in the past guarantees your resurrection in the future, the assurance of your resurrection in the future transforms the life you are living in the present.

---

[202] 1 Peter 1:3-9.
[203] Fanny Crosby, "Blessed Assurance," 1873.

Easter Sunday

What do we say on Easter Sunday?
"Christ is Risen!" ("He is Risen, indeed!")
Well, because of that—if you believe *that*—*you* are risen!
You are risen, indeed!

Acts 10:34-43 ESV

^{34} So Peter opened his mouth and said: "Truly I understand that God shows no partiality, ^{35} but in every nation anyone who fears him and does what is right is acceptable to him. ^{36} As for the word that he sent to Israel, preaching good news of peace through Jesus Christ (he is Lord of all), ^{37} you yourselves know what happened throughout all Judea, beginning from Galilee after the baptism that John proclaimed:^{38} how God anointed Jesus of Nazareth with the Holy Spirit and with power. He went about doing good and healing all who were oppressed by the devil, for God was with him. ^{39} And we are witnesses of all that he did both in the country of the Jews and in Jerusalem. They put him to death by hanging him on a tree, ^{40} but God raised him on the third day and made him to appear, ^{41} not to all the people but to us who had been chosen by God as witnesses, who ate and drank with him after he rose from the dead. ^{42} And he commanded us to preach to the people and to testify that he is the one appointed by God to be judge of the living and the dead. ^{43} To him all the prophets bear witness that everyone who believes in him receives forgiveness of sins through his name."

Coming to Life—Again

Luke 24:1-11 ESV

¹ But on the first day of the week, at early dawn, they went to the tomb, taking the spices they had prepared. ² And they found the stone rolled away from the tomb, ³ but when they went in they did not find the body of the Lord Jesus. ⁴ While they were perplexed about this, behold, two men stood by them in dazzling apparel. ⁵ And as they were frightened and bowed their faces to the ground, the men said to them, "Why do you seek the living among the dead? ⁶ He is not here, but has risen. Remember how he told you, while he was still in Galilee, ⁷ that the Son of Man must be delivered into the hands of sinful men and be crucified and on the third day rise." ⁸ And they remembered his words, ⁹ and returning from the tomb they told all these things to the eleven and to all the rest. ¹⁰ Now it was Mary Magdalene and Joanna and Mary the mother of James and the other women with them who told these things to the apostles, ¹¹ but these words seemed to them an idle tale, and they did not believe them.

26.

Coming to Life—Again

Acts 10:34-43; Luke 24:1-11 ESV

If you're here today, you probably know the story that brought us *all* here today. But maybe you don't, so let me summarize—since it's a story that loses nothing in the retelling.

A man named Jesus, Who lived in the Middle East many years ago, was arrested and killed—brutally executed—by the political authorities of His day, at the insistence of the religious authorities, because He claimed divine authority—representing Himself as the unique representative of God.

He had gathered a following by talking about God in a remarkable way, and doing things in the Name of God that were very hard to explain without assuming God had given Him the power to do them.

Those who supported this Jesus were convinced that He was God's gift to the world—God's Messiah. Those who opposed Him saw Him as a menace to *their* world, a problem to be eliminated—which they arranged.

That's the basic story, a story about real life and stuff that happened to real people.

Now, if that were the end of the story, it wouldn't be much of a story and not one that we would likely still be telling today.

Coming to Life—Again

But there's more to the story, and that "more" makes it the most important story ever told, and the most important story that will ever *be* told for as long as stories *are* told.

You see, this man Jesus was killed—by men who knew their business and performed it on Him with merciless indifference until He was as dead as you could make somebody. And then, on the third day after they killed Him, He came back to life again. And that makes for a story worth telling—again and again and again.

The people who first told the story of His coming back to life after He was killed were some of the people who followed Him and heard the stories He told them *before* He was killed. The people who killed Him—and the people who arranged for Him to be killed—didn't tell the story, and didn't believe it—because they didn't see what His supporters saw. They didn't see this Man, Jesus, come to life again.

They didn't want to believe the story, or see Jesus come back to life. It was the people who saw Jesus come to life again—and were thrilled by what they saw—who told the story—first.

And they told the story we're telling now—for two reasons. The first is that they saw Jesus after He came to life again—which tends to be pretty convincing and motivating to those who see such things. And the other reason is that one of the things Jesus told them before He was killed is that He *would* be killed, and that *after* He was killed, He would come back to life—as they discovered He had.

And that's what they told people: Jesus was killed and He came back to life, and *He* knew He was going to come back to life even before *they* knew He was going to be killed.

For somebody—anybody—to die—really die and be very, totally dead—and then come to life again three days later—is enough to start the witnesses of all that telling the story. If you saw a dead man come back to life, it would be hard to stop you from telling that story. And plenty of people tried to stop those who saw Jesus come back to life from saying so, but with very little success.

Seeing a dead man come to life is a story worth telling. It might even be enough to keep a story going—maybe even forever.

ॐ

But people who *didn't* see it (and don't want to) are likely to get tired of hearing the story. They may just want to shut the tellers of this story up. But how do you do that when the tellers seem so determined to tell—and keep on telling—the story you don't want to hear?

You could threaten them. That would intimidate the more fearful. You could lock them up. That would restrict the story to anyone locked up with them—and with the story. You could challenge the truth of the story or undermine the credibility of those telling it.

And that's been tried. It's tried a lot these days, and has shown a lot of success in suppressing the telling of the story in our times.

Today, the "anti-story" people say the story can't be true. Dead people—really, truly, totally dead people—don't come to life again. They can't. Science has proven that. So anybody who would tell the story today has to be really dumb—and maybe even dangerous.

And so, many people who know the story and believe the story and might be inclined to tell the story—don't, because they would just "die" if somebody thought they were dumb. And it could be dangerous to be thought "dangerous" today.

Are the storytellers dangerous—those who tell the story of the coming back to life of Jesus?

They are—at the same time—the *least* dangerous—and the *most* dangerous—people in the world—to the world that doesn't want to hear the story or have it told to anyone else. Those who tell the story of Jesus and His Resurrection are the most likely to be like Him in attitude and behavior.

Jesus loved His enemies and offered His betrayer a token of deep friendship.[204] Jesus turned the other cheek when attacked, and forgave stuff most folks would think unforgivable.[205] He taught the storytellers to be like gentle lambs and doves even among the wolves of the world.[206]

Those who tell the story of Jesus are the least dangerous people in the world—and the most dangerous, because of the power of the story to turn the world of anyone who will listen and believe it upside down.

But let's go back to the accusation that the tellers of the story of Jesus coming back to life are dumb because dead people can't come back to life.

Now the basis for declaring that dead people can't come to life again is that nobody has—and that "science," broadly defined, says they can't.

But by that same logic, dead people *can* come back to life if someone *has*. And if Someone *has* come to life again after being dead, who is dumber: the person who believes it, or the person who refuses to believe it, despite the evidence?

And then there's the "scientific argument," often advocated most strongly by those with the least scientific aptitude. But even if "science" says that people can't come back to life, what they mean is that science hasn't figured out how to make people come back to life, and science can't explain how it could happen if it depended solely on the capabilities science possesses or understands.

It is true that people don't come to life again under laboratory conditions—in the kinds of controlled environments that science is careful to establish and maintain.

But there are limits to what science can do and limits to what science knows.

---

[204] John 13:26.
[205] Luke 23:34.
[206] Matthew 10:16.

And then there is "beyond the limits of science." I suspect that is where resurrections take place.

༄

Jesus was killed and He came back to life and people saw Him alive after He was dead, and that's the story they told, and we are still telling today. But as I said earlier, there's more to the story.

Because Jesus came to life again after He had been killed—everything He said and everything He did before He was killed came to life again also, in a way that nobody but Jesus could have understood before His Resurrection. And that's part of the story we tell.

And because Jesus came to life again, those who saw it, and those of us who believe what they told us about it, realize that He wasn't just a man who lived in the Middle East many years ago. He wasn't just another victim of heartless, overwhelming power. He wasn't even just a unique representative of God. He was—and is—God. And that's what makes the story we tell the most important story ever told.

༄

But there's still more to the story. You see, the story isn't just about Jesus coming to life again, as wonderful and miraculous as that is. Yes, hooray for Jesus!

But the rest of the story is that everyone who hears and believes the story comes to life again, too. It is the story of the women, who went to the graveyard that Sunday morning to look for the dead Body of Jesus, with hearts just as dead, hearing the story from whomever that was who told them that Jesus was risen and alive again.

It is the story of Simon Peter, dead in his denial shame,[207] hearing the story from the women and going to see, and hearing it

---

[207] Matthew 26:69-75.

Coming to Life—Again

again from Jesus Himself, and coming to life again as the leading teller of the story at Pentecost.

And it is your story, all of you who have told me that you have never been more alive than you are now in your relationship with a Jesus Who has never been more alive to you.

It is your story. *"Christ has been raised from the dead, the first fruits of those who have fallen asleep"*[208]—and those who have heard and believed this remarkable, most important story ever told. *"For as in Adam all die, so also in Christ all will be made alive."*[209]

Paul told the story this way: *"I delivered to you as of first importance what I also received* (I told you the most important story ever told that was told to me), *that Christ died for our sins… that he was buried, that he was raised on the third day… and that he appeared to Cephas* (that's Peter), *then to the twelve.*

"Then he appeared to more than five hundred brothers at one time.… Then he appeared to James, then to all the apostles. Last of all… he appeared also to me.…"[210]

And here you may just want to pencil in to your Bible: "and to me."

"But science—!"

Never mind science.

"But nobody in his right mind could believe that someone could die and be buried and come to life again."

Nobody in his right mind should disbelieve the witnesses who saw Jesus and talked to Him and ate with Him after He died and came back to life—when life—here and hereafter—is at stake.

You've heard the story, and because you have believed it, you are coming to life again—you have come to life in this world and you will come to life in the next—with Jesus.

---

[208] 1 Corinthians 15:20, ESV.
[209] 1 Corinthians 15:22, ESV.
[210] 1 Corinthians 15:3-8, ESV.

If you believe it, it's now your story. And if it's your story, it's your story to tell, so that those who hear your story—the most important story you will ever tell—may come to life again, too.

☙❧

Easter Sunday

Luke 24:13-49 ESV

[13] That very day two of them were going to a village named Emmaus, about seven miles from Jerusalem, [14] and they were talking with each other about all these things that had happened. [15] While they were talking and discussing together, Jesus himself drew near and went with them. [16] But their eyes were kept from recognizing him. [17] And he said to them, "What is this conversation that you are holding with each other as you walk?" And they stood still, looking sad. [18] Then one of them, named Cleopas, answered him, "Are you the only visitor to Jerusalem who does not know the things that have happened there in these days?" [19] And he said to them, "What things?" And they said to him, "Concerning Jesus of Nazareth, a man who was a prophet mighty in deed and word before God and all the people, [20] and how our chief priests and rulers delivered him up to be condemned to death, and crucified him. [21] But we had hoped that he was the one to redeem Israel. Yes, and besides all this, it is now the third day since these things happened. [22] Moreover, some women of our company amazed us. They were at the tomb early in the morning, [23] and when they did not find his body, they came back saying that they had even seen a vision of angels, who said that he was alive. [24] Some of those who were with us went to the tomb and found it just as the women had said, but him they did not see." [25] And he said to them, "O foolish ones, and slow of heart to believe all that the prophets have spoken! [26] Was it not necessary that the Christ should suffer these things and enter into his glory?" [27] And beginning with Moses and all the Prophets, he interpreted to them in all the Scriptures the things concerning himself.

[28] So they drew near to the village to which they were going. He acted as if he were going farther, [29] but they urged him strongly, saying, "Stay with us, for it is toward evening and the day is now far spent." So he went in to stay with them. [30] When he was at table with them, he took the bread and blessed and broke it and gave it to them. [31] And their eyes were opened, and they recognized him.

And he vanished from their sight. [32] They said to each other, "Did not our hearts burn within us while he talked to us on the road, while he opened to us the Scriptures?" [33] And they rose that same hour and returned to Jerusalem.

Hope, Grief and Joy

And they found the eleven and those who were with them gathered together, ³⁴ saying, "The Lord has risen indeed, and has appeared to Simon!" ³⁵ Then they told what had happened on the road, and how he was known to them in the breaking of the bread.

³⁶ As they were talking about these things, Jesus himself stood among them, and said to them, "Peace to you!" ³⁷ But they were startled and frightened and thought they saw a spirit. ³⁸ And he said to them, "Why are you troubled, and why do doubts arise in your hearts? ³⁹ See my hands and my feet, that it is I myself. Touch me, and see. For a spirit does not have flesh and bones as you see that I have." ⁴⁰ And when he had said this, he showed them his hands and his feet. ⁴¹ And while they still disbelieved for joy and were marveling, he said to them, "Have you anything here to eat?" ⁴² They gave him a piece of broiled fish, ⁴³ and he took it and ate before them.

⁴⁴ Then he said to them, "These are my words that I spoke to you while I was still with you, that everything written about me in the Law of Moses and the Prophets and the Psalms must be fulfilled." ⁴⁵ Then he opened their minds to understand the Scriptures, ⁴⁶ and said to them, "Thus it is written, that the Christ should suffer and on the third day rise from the dead, ⁴⁷ and that repentance and forgiveness of sins should be proclaimed in his name to all nations, beginning from Jerusalem. ⁴⁸ You are witnesses of these things. ⁴⁹ And behold, I am sending the promise of my Father upon you. But stay in the city until you are clothed with power from on high."

27.

Hope, Grief and Joy

Luke 24:13-49 ESV

I feel sorry for people who are not here, in this room, right now—because this is, in all likelihood, the happiest place in town today.[211] Every church, in this and every town, is filled today with people who have come out to celebrate, or at least commemorate, Easter. But for you, it is different. You know something they don't know.

This is your first Easter as a new fellowship, and you are here together because, like the first disciples that very first Easter of all, you have experienced the power of the Resurrection personally, and you have the joy to prove it. And you know—beyond a shadow of a doubt—that this is the place to be. You can't imagine being anywhere else—with anybody else.

If you are a guest in this hotel, or a friend brought along by some of these joyful and excited people, or someone who saw an ad in the paper and decided to come and see what all the fuss was

---

[211] This sermon was preached to several hundred people who, just a few weeks before, had felt it necessary to withdraw from the church of which they had been members. Within days, they decided to form a new church, and three Sundays later, they met together in a rented hotel ballroom to celebrate Easter.

about, you may need a little explanation. But to explain properly, we'll need to go back a week—and almost 2,000 years.

A week takes us back to Palm Sunday, and the 2,000 years or so takes us back to Jesus Himself, riding that little donkey up the steep and crowded road to Jerusalem. The altitude is high and the hopes of His followers were even higher.

Every day, something new and wonderful seemed to be happening, wherever Jesus went. For months, He had been healing the sick[212] and feeding the poor[213] and putting the proud to shame[214] with His unconventional, but compelling, words about God. And week by week, the crowds grew, in number and excitement, as people told people how wonderful it was to follow Jesus.

And then, finally, Jesus and His following entered Jerusalem, the holy city of God, to celebrate the Passover, the holiday that got them hoping even more.

But not everybody shared their hope. There were those who did not join the parade. There were those who had a very different agenda from the one Jesus was preaching. And with stunning swiftness, the high hopes of the followers of Jesus were destroyed by powerful forces arrayed against Him. With cold and calculated cruelty, Jesus was arrested, tried, tortured and killed. His Body and the hopes of His disciples were nailed to a cross where He and their hopes suffered and died together. And in place of their hope there was shock and a sense of futility—and heart-crushing grief.

Usually, when hope is shattered, those who shared that hope are scattered. People say that "misery loves company," but that's not really true. Those who are truly miserable want to be alone. Human interaction is too hard; it requires too much energy and attentiveness to others when all your mind can think about is the cause and pain of your grief.

---

[212] Matthew 4:24.
[213] Matthew 15:32-38.
[214] Matthew 23:1-36.

And that's why two of the heartbroken disciples of Jesus left the others as soon as the Jewish Sabbath laws would let them, and headed home to a town called Emmaus. They left their familiar fellowship with hopes crushed and dreams destroyed, just to get away from whatever would remind them of their grief.

True misery wants no company, but it does need therapy. Grief needs to be processed to minimize the damage it can do to heart and mind and spirit. So as they walked away, they talked about their grief with each other—and with a Stranger Who joined them on the road.

For these disciples, this was a familiar road. They had traveled it before. But this time, the journey from Jerusalem to Emmaus was a Via Dolorosa for them—a Way of Grief. The crucifixion of their beloved Jesus was an emotional cross almost too heavy for them to bear. And so, all they could see was their incomprehensible loss—and the pain and sorrow that welled up out of it—which is probably why they gave no credence to stories back in Jerusalem of an empty tomb or of angels announcing a Resurrection. And that may also have been why the Man Who was matching them stride for stride on the dusty road aroused no sense of recognition.

The Man walking with them saw their grief and asked them about it. They told Him what they had hoped for—and why—and how their hopes had come to grief.

And then the Stranger did an odd thing.

He showed no sympathy and offered no words of consolation. He didn't seem to know anything about the terrible business in Jerusalem, but He had a lot to say to them about Jesus—and what the Bible had to say about Jesus. It was as though He saw everything they experienced in a completely different way.

And then they got to their home and invited the Stranger in. And when He joined them around their table, *they* saw something that made *them* experience everything in a completely different way, too. They saw that the Stranger was Jesus.

They saw that the dead Man on the cross was now the living Man, blessing and breaking bread, and giving it to them in the old familiar way. The Man they wanted to be the Redeemer of Israel was *not* gone forever. He was right there with them—with them *again*. And even though He disappeared as soon as they recognized Him—experienced Him—it was enough. They knew Jesus was alive because they had experienced Him in person. The Apostle Paul puts it this way: *"...that I may to know [Christ] and the power of his resurrection...."*[215]

They had known Jesus in life and had placed their hope in Him. They had seen Jesus in death and known the grief that kills hope. Now, they knew Jesus Christ Resurrected and the power of His Resurrection that not only overpowered death itself, but destroyed their grief as completely as their grief had destroyed their hope. And where grief had broken their hearts, joy now filled them.

Unlike grief, joy really does love company. The poor woman who found her lost coin called in her friends to celebrate with her.[216] The father whose prodigal son came home threw a massive party because his son had been given up for dead and turned up alive.[217] And these two disciples, who just hours earlier just had to get away from the other disciples, couldn't wait a minute to rush back to be with them—to share their unbelievable joy. What had been the Way of Grief now became the Way of Rejoicing.

Now that they had experienced the Resurrection—not just heard somebody talking about it, but experienced it—experienced the Risen Christ—for themselves—they wanted to be—*had* to be—with the other followers of Jesus—those who had experienced what they had experienced.

You see, though faith is given by God as a gift to individuals, it immediately creates community. And when they came together in the knowledge of their experience of the Resurrection, these

---

[215] Philippians 3:10, ESV.
[216] Luke 15:8-10.
[217] Luke 15:20-24.

Easter Sunday

disciples experienced His presence again. And their joy increased more and more.

That's what happens when you experience the presence of Jesus and know the power of His Resurrection—personally. That's what happened to you who have formed this new fellowship. Not so long ago, your hopes were high as you witnessed the wonderful workings of God all around you. You saw worship that was enriching and Bible studies transforming lives. You took part in ministries that met important needs and blessed many people, here and around the world. You just knew there was more to come. You were filled with high hopes.

And then, with remarkable speed, all your hopes came crashing down. Dreams gave way to despair and grief. So much lost! And where to go? What to do? How to tell people what happened? And is there any point? Maybe you should just go home. Take your grief and go away. Suffer quietly and alone.

ò§

But here you are, less than a month later—the happiest people in town. Here you are, a Christian fellowship meeting in hotels and schools and "wherever" because you have no church facilities. You also have no furnishings, or equipment, or supplies. Yes, you do, finally, have donuts, but three weeks ago, you didn't even have a name.

Why are you here? Why are you so excited about being here? Why are you so thrilled to be together, wherever you are?

Why? Because, in the deepest, darkest moment of grief—a grief that wiped out your greatest hope—you experienced the miracle of the Resurrection *personally*—you encountered the Risen Christ Who came to you, and in the process, gave you an inexplicable and divine joy that wiped away your grief as completely and unexpectedly as that grief had wiped away your hope. Your hope was real, and when it was destroyed, your grief was real. And when Jesus took away your grief and restored your hope, your joy was real—*is* real.

And the joy is so wonderful that you want to be with people who have experienced the same thing—who know what you know—who know Jesus in the way you now know Him—in all the power of His miraculous Resurrection. Once you've seen Jesus—and He's here, whether you recognize Him or not—but once you've seen Jesus—once He's revealed Himself to you in the breaking of bread or the opening of the scriptures or simply in the joy of your fellowship together, you won't be happy sitting home alone in your personal Emmaus.

That we are here today, together, is a miracle. That we, of all people, are overwhelmed—not by grief, but by joy—is a miracle—a Resurrection miracle. We have walked the Emmaus Road, in grief first and then in joy. And we are one, united in the power of our Risen Christ Who came to us in our grief and replaced that grief with an indestructible joy.

And if you are a guest in the hotel, or a friend of the family, or someone who just decided to check us out, the miracle is yours, too, if you want it. Not because we say so, but because Jesus will accept any invitation to come in.[218]

If He is a Stranger to you, don't worry. He will reveal Himself to you even as He has to us. That's the purpose of the Resurrection. What we tell you about our experience may not impress you, but when you experience the reality and power of the Resurrection for yourself, the shattered hopes and crushing grief of your life will be replaced by His all-surpassing joy.

You could be the happiest person in town—or one of them, along with everyone else in this room.

---

[218] Revelation 3:20.

The Sunday After Easter

Unless I See Him

John 20:19-31 NRSV

¹⁹ When it was evening on that day, the first day of the week, and the doors of the house where the disciples had met were locked for fear of the Jews, Jesus came and stood among them and said, "Peace be with you." ²⁰ After he said this, he showed them his hands and his side. Then the disciples rejoiced when they saw the Lord. ²¹ Jesus said to them again, "Peace be with you. As the Father has sent me, so I send you." ²² When he had said this, he breathed on them and said to them, "Receive the Holy Spirit. ²³ If you forgive the sins of any, they are forgiven them; if you retain the sins of any, they are retained."

²⁴ But Thomas (who was called the Twin), one of the twelve, was not with them when Jesus came. ²⁵ So the other disciples told him, "We have seen the Lord." But he said to them, "Unless I see the mark of the nails in his hands, and put my finger in the mark of the nails and my hand in his side, I will not believe."

²⁶ A week later his disciples were again in the house, and Thomas was with them. Although the doors were shut, Jesus came and stood among them and said, "Peace be with you." ²⁷ Then he said to Thomas, "Put your finger here and see my hands. Reach out your hand and put it in my side. Do not doubt but believe." ²⁸ Thomas answered him, "My Lord and my God!" ²⁹ Jesus said to him, "Have you believed because you have seen me? Blessed are those who have not seen and yet have come to believe."

³⁰ Now Jesus did many other signs in the presence of his disciples, which are not written in this book. ³¹ But these are written so that you may come to believe that Jesus is the Messiah, the Son of God, and that through believing you may have life in his name.

28.

Unless I See Him

John 20:19-31 NRSV

I have some recollection that last Sunday was Easter. You remember: Mary Magdalene came to the garden early on that particular Sunday and got a nasty surprise—followed by a glorious surprise.

Peter and John got cardiovascular workouts soon thereafter, racing to the graveyard, and then had some sort of religious experience, once they got a look inside the empty tomb. But then they seemed to have forgotten the whole thing in favor of a little quiet time in the security and seclusion of a Jerusalem safe house.

Later that day—that first Easter Sunday—as day gave way to night, Jesus appeared to His disciples in a place and in a way they did not expect. He appeared for a reason, of course: to foster faith in His beleaguered followers.

John writes that Jesus came to them (which can be a little disconcerting when you have made very sure that all the doors and windows are shut and locked).

John says Jesus stood with them—in the midst of them—which points to the certainty of a face-to-face encounter. It also suggests the solidarity Jesus shared with them: they were in trouble—because of Jesus—and Jesus appeared to them, despite their precautions to keep everyone but themselves out.

But His purpose was not to scare them; it was to demonstrate to them how unimportant their fears were—if they followed Someone Who had been raised from the dead. He breathed on them and they received the Holy Spirit—according to John's account. Jesus provided empirical evidence as to both His crucifixion and His resurrection that would answer some of their questions—and raise more. And He gave them—delegated to them—the power and authority to accomplish the job He would put at the top of their "to do" list: *"Go...and make disciples...."*[219]

The appearance of Jesus "did the job" for those who were there: they believed. But the news of their encounter with Jesus wasn't enough for the disciple who wasn't there.

Thomas wasn't hanging out that day with what was left of the Twelve that Jesus had chosen to begin and become the New Israel. Thomas had not seen and heard what they had, and he wasn't impressed with their report of what had impressed them. Thomas spelled out very clearly to the other disciples what it would take for him to believe that Jesus was alive.

༄༅

Funny thing, though: when he finally saw Jesus, the requirements Thomas had demanded just didn't seem necessary any more. He wouldn't jump on their bandwagon—believe the most incredible thing in the world—just on their say-so. But when *he* saw Jesus as *they* had seen Jesus—when *he* heard Jesus as *they* had heard Jesus—Thomas was ready to believe what the rest had known for a week already: Jesus was alive—Jesus was risen from the dead—Jesus is Lord and God.

Thomas did not believe in the Resurrection because somebody—or even a bunch of somebodies—told him that Jesus

---

[219] Matthew 28:19, ESV.

had been raised from the dead. He *believed* in Jesus because he had a personal *encounter* with Jesus, Who was supposed to be dead, but was alive instead.

He did not believe because of what they told him. But because they told Thomas what they believed and why, he chose to be at a place where he could encounter Jesus and discover the truth for himself—and believe in Jesus for himself.

And so it is, even today. Your testimony—your experience—will not bring others to faith in Jesus. But your story—and your faith—may draw a modern-day "Thomas" to a place where the Risen Christ will visit him or her as He visited you. It took the disciples a week to get Thomas where he needed to be to meet the Risen Christ. It may take you a day or a decade or a lifetime to get someone else to that place.

Whatever it takes—it's what Jesus wants you to do. That's why He told the disciples (and tells us), "*As the Father has sent me, so send I you.*" He wants to encounter all the "Thomases" He can.

And once the first (and adamantly faithless) Thomas met the Risen Christ, *that* Thomas changed his mind about what they had told him. They got *that* Thomas where Jesus wanted him, and Jesus did the rest.

That's how it worked then—and that's how it works now.

For Want of a Resurrection…

1 Corinthians 15:1-22 ESV

¹ Now I would remind you, brothers, of the gospel I preached to you, which you received, in which you stand, ² and by which you are being saved, if you hold fast to the word I preached to you—unless you believed in vain.

³ For I delivered to you as of first importance what I also received: that Christ died for our sins in accordance with the Scriptures, ⁴ that he was buried, that he was raised on the third day in accordance with the Scriptures, ⁵ and that he appeared to Cephas, then to the twelve. ⁶ Then he appeared to more than five hundred brothers at one time, most of whom are still alive, though some have fallen asleep. ⁷ Then he appeared to James, then to all the apostles. ⁸ Last of all, as to one untimely born, he appeared also to me. ⁹ For I am the least of the apostles, unworthy to be called an apostle, because I persecuted the church of God. ¹⁰ But by the grace of God I am what I am, and his grace toward me was not in vain. On the contrary, I worked harder than any of them, though it was not I, but the grace of God that is with me. ¹¹ Whether then it was I or they, so we preach and so you believed.

¹² Now if Christ is proclaimed as raised from the dead, how can some of you say that there is no resurrection of the dead? ¹³ But if there is no resurrection of the dead, then not even Christ has been raised. ¹⁴ And if Christ has not been raised, then our preaching is in vain and your faith is in vain. ¹⁵ We are even found to be misrepresenting God, because we testified about God that he raised Christ, whom he did not raise if it is true that the dead are not raised. ¹⁶ For if the dead are not raised, not even Christ has been raised. ¹⁷ And if Christ has not been raised, your faith is futile and you are still in your sins. ¹⁸ Then those also who have fallen asleep in Christ have perished. ¹⁹ If in Christ we have hope in this life only, we are of all people most to be pitied.

²⁰ But in fact Christ has been raised from the dead, the firstfruits of those who have fallen asleep. ²¹ For as by a man came death, by a man has come also the resurrection of the dead. ²² For as in Adam all die, so also in Christ shall all be made alive.

29.

For Want of a Resurrection…

1 Corinthians 15:1-22; John 20:19-31 ESV (p. 212)

There is a nursery rhyme that has been around for hundreds of years (in one form or another) that traces a massive disaster back to a seemingly insignificant detail. The initial, insignificant detail is the loss of a horseshoe nail. But this minor inconvenience causes other, cascading problems—and before you know it—without imagining it possible—the greatest catastrophe befalls. One version of the verse goes like this:

> For want of a nail the shoe was lost.
> For want of a shoe the horse was lost.
> For want of a horse the rider was lost.
> For want of a rider the battle was lost.
> For want of a victory the kingdom was lost.
> And all for the want of a nail.[220]

The kingdom was lost—all for the want of a nail.
Now, hold that thought—we'll come back to it.

---

[220] Quoted by Benjamin Franklin in *Poor Richard's Almanac* in 1758.

For Want of a Resurrection...

Chapter 15 of First Corinthians is no nursery rhyme, but the Apostle Paul is engaged in a little "one thing leads to another" discussion in its verses. He begins, not with the loss of a horseshoe nail, but with an unwillingness of some people to believe something—the unwillingness of some of the Christians in the Corinthian church to believe in the resurrection of the dead.

You wouldn't think that what a group of people believes—or doesn't believe—would be that important. It's just an idea—an attitude—a perspective. And we're not talking about a lot of people—or anybody very important, in the grand scheme of things. At least, that's how it seems.

But to hear Paul tell it, a lot more than a kingdom will be lost—all for the want of a belief in the resurrection of the dead: *"...if there is no resurrection of the dead, then not even Christ has been raised. And if Christ has not been raised, then our preaching is in vain and your faith is in vain.... We are...misrepresenting God...the dead are not raised...and you are still in your sins."*

A lot of people today don't believe in the idea of a resurrection from the dead—not for Jesus—not for anybody. It's an idea that just doesn't sit well with the empirical mindset that emerged in the Age of Reason. It doesn't make sense in this modern world when powerful space telescopes can't find heaven and cutting-edge CAT scans can map your body but miss your soul.

The world around us is systematically dismantling all the evidence of the witnesses of the Resurrection of Jesus. Sacred words are erased from civic buildings, prohibited from being there by law. Public expressions of faith in the Resurrection are also banned from societal gatherings, and private expressions are viciously attacked as hateful and harmful to the common good.

Even in the broad community of individuals who still identify themselves as Christians, more and more folks are concluding that identifying themselves with the idea of a bodily resurrection is intellectually indefensible and theologically unnecessary. Many who maintain an affiliation with a church today do so merely to promote some generic form of good behavior and to enjoy the emotional and commercial benefits of some occasional religious activity. Their approach: embrace what you feel comfortable with in the biblical witness about Jesus and distance yourself (quietly or otherwise) from the rest.

To the world, the Resurrection isn't really that important. To the world, it isn't real at all. It's a fairy tale no more significant or relevant to life than a nail from a horse's shoe.

"People aren't resurrected. Resurrections don't happen. That's not how the world works."

Today, we know better than the Bible, it seems.

But don't be too fast in ascribing this attitude just to the infinitely greater sophistication of the *modern* mind. They were saying this sort of stuff—in churches—within decades of the Resurrection itself, while plenty of eyewitnesses were still around to confirm they had seen Jesus alive after His Crucifixion. People were "putting down" the Resurrection in the church in Corinth within months (or weeks?) of Paul himself sharing the gospel of salvation with them, including, no doubt, his own testimony of his personal encounter with the Risen Christ.

Wanting to wriggle out of believing the Resurrection is nothing new. As Paul's argument indicates, Christians were already trying to dismiss the Resurrection before most of the books in the New Testament had been written.

And ever since, there have been two kinds of people in the world: those who do not believe in the Resurrection—and those who do...

❧

...which brings us back to the nursery rhyme about the horseshoe nail.

Those people—in the church and out—who do *not* believe in the Resurrection are living their lives amid a process not unlike the one described in the children's tale. They are missing something.

For Want of a Resurrection...

To them, it seems like nothing—completely insignificant. But because they do not believe in the Resurrection—because they do not "have" the Resurrection as a part of their lives—they do not have something else.

They do not have the power of the living Christ available to—and active in—their lives. After all, if you do not believe that Jesus has been raised from the dead, you're not going to believe that He is alive now. And you're not really going to believe that He can love you or protect you or guide you as you go about the business of living your life each day.

All you can do is wrap your thoughts, your decisions, your values and your actions in a mantle of "Christian respectability." All you have is *your* power, or that of other people—*your* wisdom, or that of other people—*your* sense of right and wrong, or that of the people around you. But for want of the Resurrection, the Risen Christ is lost to you. All you're left with is whatever religious fervor or feelings you can generate on your own or with the help of those other people.

And for want of the Risen Christ, a genuine, living relationship with Him is lost to you. And if you have no relationship with the living Christ, the power He would give you is lost to you as well. And if you cannot receive His power, you cannot know the hope that comes from it. And if you lack the divine hope that grows out of your experiencing the power of the Risen Christ, you lose out on the peace that passes understanding[221] and the joy that knows no end.[222]

How did Paul put it?

"...if there is no resurrection of the dead...your faith is in vain."

But that's not all.

"...if there is no resurrection of the dead...you are still in your sins."

For want of the Resurrection, you have no assurance of salvation—no *hope* of salvation.

---

[221] Philippians 4:7.
[222] John 16:22-24.

The Sunday After Easter

When the nail was lost, it triggered a chain reaction that ended in the loss of an earthy kingdom. For want of faith in the Resurrection, the end-result is your losing the glorious place that could have been yours—*would* have been yours—in the eternal kingdom of God.

On the other hand, there are those silly, misguided, dim-witted people who *do* believe in the Resurrection of the dead today—people like—well—you and me.

If you believe, as the Bible teaches, that God raised Jesus from the dead—so that Jesus lives forever as the eternal King of kings—your faith is not in theological ideas, but in a living Person. Because you believe Jesus lives, you are open to His divine, redemptive interaction with you. Because you are open in faith to the involvement of the living Lord in your life, you experience the impact of His active power in your life.

This miraculous power you experience gives you a reason and the confidence to hope in His promises to bless you and keep you, in this life and the next. Being able to believe that the living Jesus has saved you from the condemnation of sin by His death, and is sustaining you—forever—by His infinite power and love, makes incredible joy possible, whatever the burdens this life may bring.

You're looking at two totally different kinds of life when you compare the person who believes in the Resurrection with the person who doesn't. If you don't believe me, look at Thomas, the Apostle, before and after He saw the Risen Christ.

For a week after the Resurrection, Thomas did not believe Jesus had been raised, even though the other disciples assured him it was so. For a week, Jesus remained dead to Thomas.

Thomas had no sense of the power of the Resurrection. He was closed to the power of Jesus. He had no hope. He had no joy. He was dead inside because he could not believe that Jesus was not dead. That was his life—for a week.

And then, Thomas saw Jesus—alive. Thomas became one who had not believed the Resurrection and then did. His darkness

For Want of a Resurrection...

turned to light. His helplessness was replaced with power. His hopelessness evaporated and joy poured in to take its place.

In the upper room at the Last Supper, Thomas had complained to the soon to be crucified Jesus, *"Lord, we do not know where you are going. How can we know the way?"*[223]

In this locked-up room with the Risen Jesus, Thomas knows immediately everything he needs to know. His life has just gone from "over" to over-joyed: *"My Lord and my God!"*

Everything he thought he had lost when he did not believe in the Resurrection, Thomas discovered that he gained the moment he did believe in it.

"But Thomas *saw* Jesus. And Paul *saw* Jesus. The eyewitnesses all *saw* Jesus, raised from the dead."

And if you believe in the Resurrection, you will, too. You will see the impact of His power *in* your life. You will see the influence of His love *on* your life. You will see the miracles of His grace *throughout* your life. You will see the confirmation of your faith in ways the world (and maybe even you) cannot understand. You will see His kingdom coming and your place in it—a place you had lost because of your sin, and regained because of your faith in the One Who died to restore it to you.

If you believe in the Resurrection, you will be a witness to it. You will see Jesus, time and time again—alive—resurrected and reigning. If you "nail down" your belief in the resurrection of the dead—and the Resurrection of Jesus Christ—all that might have been lost to you will be safe and secured forever.

---

[223] John 14:5, ESV.

Indices

Sermon Titles in Alphabetical Order

Title	Page
A Meal to Remember	35
A Very Difficult Commandment	61
Coming to Life—Again	195
Delivery Charges	41
Easter Come and Easter Go	153
For Want of a Resurrection	217
Hanging Out with Jesus	121
Have They Taken Away Your Lord?	157
His Resurrection—and Yours	185
Hope, Grief and Joy	205
Hope in the Darkness	75
I Serve You; I Command You	57
Learning Obedience	135
Let's Try This Again	49
Life, If You Will Have It	177
Look Who's Here	25
Not Exactly What They Expected	5
Our Evil—God's Good	97

Sermon Titles in Alphabetical Order

Title	**Page**
The Believe It or Not Story	147
The Empty God	139
They Could Not Keep Him Out	15
This is Jesus	115
Today's the Day	161
Treachery at the Table	67
Trying Questions	87
Unless I See Him	213
What Does It Take…?	129
Who *Is* This Guy?	107
You Can Kill Him, But…	167

Sermon Texts in Biblical Order

Text	Title	Page

Genesis
45:1-8	Our Evil—God's Good	94
50:15-20	Our Evil—God's Good	94

Exodus
12:21-32	Delivery Charges	40

Deuteronomy
30:15-20	Life, If You Will Have It	175

2 Samuel
5:1-3, 6-7	They Could Not Keep Him Out	13
15:13-30	Hope in the Darkness	72

Isaiah
52:13-15	Who *Is* This Guy?	103
53:1-12	Who *Is* This Guy?	103

Jeremiah
31:31-34	Let's Try This Again	47

Zechariah
9:9-10	Look Who's Here	23

Matthew
21:1-11	Look Who's Here	24
27:22-31	Who *Is* This Guy?	105
27:33-54	This is Jesus	113
28:1-10	Life, If You Will Have It	176
	His Resurrection—and Yours	176

Sermon Texts in Biblical Order

Text	Title	Page
Mark		
11:1-10	Not Exactly What They Expected	4
14:32-36	Hope in the Darkness	74
Luke		
22:7-20	A Meal to Remember	34
	Delivery Charges	34
22:7-20	Let's Try This Again	48
23:1-43	Our Evil—God's Good	95
23:32-43	Hanging Out with Jesus	120
24:1-11	Coming to Life—Again	194
24:13-49	Hope, Grief and Joy	203
John		
12:12-16	They Could Not Keep Him Out	14
13:1-7; 31b-35	I Serve You; I Command You	55
	A Very Difficult Commandment	55
13:21-30	Treachery at the Table	67
18:28—19:16	Trying Questions	85
19:1-22, 28-34	What Does It Take...?	127
20:1-18	The Believe It or Not Story	146
	Easter Come and Easter Go	146
	Have They Taken Away Your Lord?	146
	Today's the Day!	146
	You Can Kill Him, But…	146
20:19-31	Unless I See Him	212
	For Want of a Resurrection…	212
Acts		
10:34-43	Coming to Life—Again	193

Sermon Texts in Biblical Order

Text	Title	Page
Romans		
6:3-11	His Resurrection—and Yours	184
1 Corinthians		
15:1-22	For Want of a Resurrection...	216
Philippians		
2:2-11	The Empty God	138
Hebrews		
5:1-10	Learning Obedience	134
1 Peter		
2:21-24	This is Jesus	113

Sermon Texts in Lectionary Order

Date	Text	Page
Cycle A		
Baptism of the Lord	Acts 10:34-43	193
Epiphany 6 [6]	Deuteronomy 30:15-20	175
Palm Sunday	Matthew 21:1-11	24
	Matthew 27:22-31	105
	Matthew 27:33-54	113
Easter Vigil	Matthew 28:1-10	176
Easter	Matthew 28:1-10	176
Easter 3	Luke 24:13-49	203
Easter 4	1 Peter 2:21-24	113
Pentecost	John 20:19-31	212
Proper 7 [12]	Romans 6:3-11	184
Proper 9 [14]	Zechariah 9:9-10	23
Proper 15 [20]	Genesis 45:1-8	94
Proper 18 [24]	Genesis 50:15-20	94
Proper 21 [26]	Philippians 2:2-11	138

Sermon Texts in Lectionary Order

Text	Title	Page
Cycle B		
Lent 5	Jeremiah 31:31-34	47
	Hebrews 5:1-10	134
Palm Sunday	Mark 11:1-10	4
	Mark 14:32-36	74
	John 12:12-16	14
Easter	1 Corinthians 15:1-22	216
Proper 9 [14]	2 Samuel 5:1-3, 6-7	13
Proper 24 [29]	Hebrews 5:1-10	134
Cycle C		
Epiphany 5 [5]	1 Corinthians 15:1-22	216
Epiphany 6 [6]	1 Corinthians 15:1-22	216
Epiphany 7 [7]	Genesis 45:1-8	94
Palm Sunday	Luke 22:7-20	34, 48
	Luke 23:1-4, 20-26, 34-43	95
Eater Vigil	Luke 24:1-11	194
Easter	Luke 24:1-11	194
	1 Corinthians 15:1-22	216

Sermon Texts in Lectionary Order

Text	Title	Page

Cycle C (Continued)

Proper 18 [23]	Deuteronomy 30:15-20	175
Proper 24 [29]	Jeremiah 31:31-34	47
Reign of Christ [34]	Luke 23:32-43	120

Cycle ABC

Holy Name	Philippians 2:2-11	138
Palm Sunday	Philippians 2:2-11	138
Holy Wednesday	John 13:21-30	67
Holy Thursday	John 13:1-7; 31b-35	55
Good Friday	Isaiah 52:13—53:12	103
	John 18:28—19:16	85
	John 19:1-22, 28-34	127
Easter Vigil	Romans 6:3-11	184
Easter	John 20:1-18	146
	Acts 10:34-43	193
Easter Evening	Luke 24:13-49	203
Easter 2	John 20:19-31	212

Additional Scriptures Referenced

Text	Title	Page
Genesis		
1:1	Life, If You Will Have It	179
1:1-2	The Empty God	139
2:5	The Believe It or Not Story	149
3	What Does It Take…?	131
3:8-9	Look Who's Here	26
Exodus		
3:12	Life, If You Will Have It	182
11-12	A Meal to Remember	36
12:29-32	Not Exactly What They Expected	6
1 Samuel		
17:1-51	The Empty God	141
1 Kings		
1:32-40	They Could Not Keep Him Out	16
Psalms		
22:1	What Does It Take…?	130
22:1	The Empty God	142
24:1	You Can Kill Him, But…	170
51:4	Our Evil—God's Good	99
Isaiah		
11	Look Who's Here	27
40:17	Delivery Charges	43
55:8-9, 11	Not Exactly What They Expected	11
60:1-2	Today's the Day!	164
60:19-20	Today's the Day!	166

Additional Scriptures Referenced

Text	Title	Page
Jeremiah		
23:5-8	Look Who's Here	27
Hosea		
11:1-2	What Does It Take…?	130
11:8	What Does It Take…?	131
Jonah		
3	Delivery Charges	43
Zechariah		
9:9-10	They Could Not Keep Him Out	18
Matthew		
3:17	Who *Is* This Guy?	110
4:24	Hope, Grief and Joy	206
5:39-41	Who *Is* This Guy?	111
9:4	You Can Kill Him, But…	171
9:10	I Serve You; I Command You	58
10:16	Coming to Life—Again	198
11:29	Who *Is* This Guy?	111
12:30	Life—If You Will Have It	179
14:25	A Very Difficult Commandment	61
15:30-31	They Could Not Keep Him Out	18
15:32-38	Hope, Grief and Joy	206
16:21	Not Exactly What They Expected	5
16:21-23	A Meal to Remember	36
16:22	Not Exactly What They Expected	5
16:23	Not Exactly What They Expected	5
18:20	Look Who's Here	30

Additional Scriptures Referenced

Text	Title	Page

Matthew (Continued)

20:28	Not Exactly What They Expected	10
21:8-9	They Could Not Keep Him Out	16
21:12	Not Exactly What They Expected	8
21:12-13	They Could Not Keep Him Out	17
23:1-36	Hope, Grief and Joy	206
23:37	What Does It Take…?	131
26:3-4	Not Exactly What They Expected	7
26:3-5	They Could Not Keep Him Out	17
26:21	Treachery at the Table	68
26:47-54	Not Exactly What They Expected	8
26:26	Treachery at the Table	68
26:69-75	Coming to Life—Again	199
27:11-14	Not Exactly What They Expected	8
27:20-21	Not Exactly What They Expected	9
27:35-43	Not Exactly What They Expected	8
27:41-43	They Could Not Keep Him Out	17
27:45	Hope in the Darkness	80
27:46	What Does It Take…?	130
28:19	Unless I See Him	214
28:20	Look Who's Here	26

Mark

5:1-15	You Can Kill Him, But…	171
8:31	You Can Kill Him, But…	168
10:35-41	A Very Difficult Commandment	64
10:46-52	Not Exactly What They Expected	6
10:46-52	They Could Not Keep Him Out	15
11:8-9	They Could Not Keep Him Out	16
11:11	They Could Not Keep Him Out	17
14:55-59	They Could Not Keep Him Out	18

Additional Scriptures Referenced

Text	Title	Page

Mark (Continued)
15:25, 33-37	They Could Not Keep Him Out	18
16:19	You Can Kill Him, But…	169

Luke
2:11	Look Who's Here	28
2:11	Look Who's Here	30
2:52	Who *Is* This Guy?	109
2:52	Learning Obedience	135
6:1-11	Not Exactly What They Expected	9
7:37-39	I Serve You; I Command You	58
8:2	You Can Kill Him, But…	167
9:22	You Can Kill Him, But…	168
9:23	Who *Is* This Guy?	111
15:8-10	Hope, Grief and Joy	208
15:20-24	Hope, Grief and Joy	208
17:10-11	I Serve You; I Command You	58
18:16-17	Not Exactly What They Expected	6
19:1-10	Not Exactly What They Expected	6
19:5	I Serve You; I Command You	58
19:37	Not Exactly What They Expected	7
19:37-38	They Could Not Keep Him Out	16
19:47-48	They Could Not Keep Him Out	17
23:34	Hope in the Darkness	80
23:34	Coming to Life—Again	198
23:39-43	This is Jesus	117

John
1:1	Who *Is* This Guy?	109
1:1-2	Look Who's Here	31
1:1-3	Look Who's Here	28

Additional Scriptures Referenced

Text	Title	Page

John (Continued)

1:1, 14	The Empty God	139
1:9-11	Look Who's Here	28
1:12-13	Today's the Day!	165
1:14	Not Exactly What They Expected	11
1:29	Look Who's Here	29
1:29	This is Jesus	118
1:40-41	Look Who's Here	30
3:3	Today's the Day!	163
3:4	Today's the Day!	163
3:16	Not Exactly What They Expected	10
3:16	Look Who's Here	28
3:16	A Very Difficult Commandment	63
6:40	His Resurrection—and Yours	187
10:10	Life, If You Will Have It	181
10:17-18	Not Exactly What They Expected	10
10:28-29	The Empty God	143
10:30	What Does It Take…?	130
11:38-44	They Could Not Keep Him Out	15
11:43	The Believe It or Not Story	151
11:43-44	A Very Difficult Commandment	61
11:45-53	You Can Kill Him, But…	167
11:47-50	Not Exactly What They Expected	9
13:26	Coming to Life—Again	198
14:5	For Want of a Resurrection…	222
16:22-24	For Want of a Resurrection…	220
16:33	Look Who's Here	29
18:1-8	Not Exactly What They Expected	8
18:33	Not Exactly What They Expected	8
18:36	Not Exactly What They Expected	8
18:36-37	Not Exactly What They Expected	10

Additional Scriptures Referenced

Text	Title	Page
John (Continued)		
19	You Can Kill Him, But…	167
19:1-3	They Could Not Keep Him Out	18
19:12-16	They Could Not Keep Him Out	18
19:15	Not Exactly What They Expected	9
19:15	This is Jesus	116
19:16-18	They Could Not Keep Him Out	17
19:21	This is Jesus	116
19:22	This is Jesus	116
19:30	You Can Kill Him, But…	167
20:19	They Could Not Keep Him Out	18
20:19-22	You Can Kill Him, But…	171
20:19-29	Today's the Day!	164
Acts		
4:12	Who *Is* This Guy?	112
10:39-40, 43	Who *Is* This Guy?	110
Romans		
5:2b-5	Hope in the Darkness	80
5:5	Hope in the Darkness	81
5:6-10	Not Exactly What They Expected	11
8:28	Look Who's Here	25
8:28	Look Who's Here	31
8:34	I Serve You; I Command You	59
10:8-9	Life—If You Will Have It	179
12:1	Delivery Charges	46
1 Corinthians		
6:14	His Resurrection—and Yours	187
11:23-25	Delivery Charges	41

Additional Scriptures Referenced

Text	Title	Page

1 Corinthians (Continued)
13:1-3	A Very Difficult Commandment	61
13:4-8	A Very Difficult Commandment	65
15:3-8	Coming to Life—Again	200
15:3-8	You Can Kill Him, But…	171
15:13-19	Life, If You Will Have It	178
15:20	Coming to Life—Again	200
15:22	The Believe It or Not Story	150
15:22	Coming to Life—Again	200
15:42-44, 52	His Resurrection—and Yours	187

2 Corinthians
4:8-9	Hope in the Darkness	79
5:21	A Meal to Remember	36
5:21	What Does It Take…?	130
5:21	What Does It Take…?	131
5:21	The Empty God	140
12:9	The Empty God	143

Galatians
4:4	Who *Is* This Guy?	108
4:4	Who *Is* This Guy?	109
6:7	Let's Try This Again	50

Ephesians
5:25	A Very Difficult Commandment	64

Philippians
2:5-8	His Resurrection—and Yours	189
2:6	Look Who's Here	28
2:6	Who *Is* This Guy?	109

Additional Scriptures Referenced

Text	Title	Page

Philippians (Continued)
2:6-7	They Could Not Keep Him Out	17
2:6-7	I Serve You; I Command You	58
2:6-7	Treachery at the Table	70
2:6-7	Who *Is* This Guy?	109
2:7	Our Evil—God's Good	101
2:7	Today's the Day!	165
2:8	Who *Is* This Guy?	109
2:9	Who *Is* This Guy?	110
2:10-11	Not Exactly What They Expected	12
2:10-11	They Could Not Keep Him Out	20
3:10	Hope, Grief and Joy	208
4:7	For Want of a Resurrection	220

Colossians
1:15-19	Who *Is* This Guy?	109
1:15-20	The Empty God	140

1 Thessalonians
4:14, 16	His Resurrection—and Yours	187

Hebrews
5:8	Who *Is* This Guy?	109
11:12	Today's the Day!	164
12:1-2	The Empty God	142
13:5	Look Who's Here	29

1 Peter
1:3	Today's the Day!	166
1:3-9	His Resurrection—and Yours	190
1:23	Today's the Day!	165

Additional Scriptures Referenced

Text	Title	Page
1 John		
5:1	Today's the Day!	165
Revelation		
3:20	They Could Not Keep Him Out	19
3:20	Hope, Grief and Joy	210
3:21	They Could Not Keep Him Out	21
11:15	Not Exactly What They Expected	11
11:15	They Could Not Keep Him Out	20
19:16	Look Who's Here	29

www.ingramcontent.com/pod-product-compliance
Lightning Source LLC
Chambersburg PA
CBHW020849090426
42736CB00008B/305